Intermediate Workbook

New
Headway
English Course

Liz & John Soars

Oxford University Press

Contents

△	Grammar explanation
T	Recording on optional cassette

Auxiliary verbs
have/have got

1 The forms of *do*, *be*, and *have*

T.1   Read the following sentences.

a I like tea.
b I don't like coffee.
c Do you like tea?
d My father likes tea.
e My mother doesn't like tea.
f Does your father like tea?

Continue the following sentences in the same way.

a I work in an office.

b _____ in a bank.

c _____

d _____

e _____

f _____

a I'm learning Spanish.

b _____ Portuguese.

c _____

d _____

e _____

f _____

a I saw the Taj Mahal.

b _____ the River Ganges.

c _____

d _____

e _____

f _____

a I've met the Queen.

b _____ Prince Charles.

c _____

d _____

e _____

f _____

2 Full verb or auxiliary verb?

Write **A** or **F** next to the following sentences to show whether *have*, *be*, or *do* is used as an **auxiliary** verb or a **full** verb.

Example

[A] Have you ever stayed at the Ritz?

[F] We had breakfast in bed.

a ☐ **Did** John give you those flowers?
b ☐ I **did** my homework very quickly last night.
c ☐ She **has** a shower every morning before school.
d ☐ We **weren't** talking to James about his exam.
e ☐ Lots of trees **were** blown down.
f ☐ Where **were** you yesterday?
g ☐ Mary never **does** the washing up.
h ☐ Thank goodness we **have** a dishwasher!
i ☐ How many people **have** you invited to the party?
j ☐ Why **are** you leaving so early?
k ☐ We've got a beautiful puppy called Molly.
l ☐ We **have** a beautiful puppy called Molly.

3 Contracted forms

Rewrite the sentences with contracted forms where they are possible.

Example
I do not know where the post office is.
*I **don't** know where the post office is.*

a She has got two brothers and she does not get on with either of them.

_____

b He has no brothers or sisters, he is an only child.

_____

c We were not interested in the film so we did not stay until the end.

_____

d He did not go to the party because he had a cold.

_____

e They are getting married when they have saved enough money.

_____

f John is not sure where Jill is.

_____

g She is feeding the dog. It is always fed at six o'clock.

_____

h I do not want them to know who I am.

_____

i Do you not understand what I am saying?

_____

j Where is the man who has been to New Zealand?

_____

4 *My computer's gone wrong!*

1 **T.2** Read the telephone conversation and put the correct auxiliary verb into each gap. Use the contracted form where possible.

D Good afternoon, Apple Helpline here. I'm Damian. How can I help you?

V Oh, at last! Hello, Damian. I (**a**) _____ got a terrible problem with my computer. It (**b**) _____ (not) working at all!

D OK, OK. Tell me your name and your company name and describe what (**c**) _____ happened.

V My name's Valerie, Val actually, Valerie Marks. I (**d**) _____ (not) work for a company, I'm self-employed. I work at home, and I (**e**) _____ trying to meet an important deadline at the moment. This morning I (**f**) _____ working away happily, when suddenly everything stopped and a message came on the screen. Then the screen went blank.

D OK Val, (**g**) _____ (not) worry! What (**h**) _____ the message say?

V I can't remember exactly, because I (**i**) _____ (not) understand it, but I think it said something about 'not enough memory'.

D It's OK, Val. I understand. Tell me, Val, (**j**) _____ you switched the computer off?

V No, I (**k**) _____ (not). It's still on.

D Fine, Val. Now do exactly what I say. Go to your computer, OK? Can you see a 'W' in the top right-hand corner? Click on that 'W' with the mouse. What (**l**) _____ it say? Can you read it to me?

V It says three things. There's a list of three things. First it says …

2 Here are some questions about the conversation. The words are mixed up. Put them in the right order. Then answer the question.

a Val the is why Apple Helpline ringing?

_____ ?

Because _____

b work for Val does company which?

_____ ?

She _____

c doing when computer she her was what stopped?

_____ ?

She _____

d Val why remember message the can't?

_____ ?

Because _____

e switched computer she has her off?

_____ ?

No, _____

5 Making questions

1 Put the words in the right order to make questions. Then answer them about yourself.

> **Example**
> parents   where   were   your   born?
> *Where were your parents born?*
> *My mother was born in Scotland and my father was born in Durham.*

a moment   what   you   at   are   the   wearing?

_____ ?

_____

b living   you   started   were   where   when   you   school?

_____ ?

_____

c go   you   where   holiday   were   did   child   when   you   on   a?

_____ ?

_____

d play   any   the   at   sports   weekend   you   do?

_____ ?

e up   time   morning   what   did   get   this   you?

_____ ?

_____

f pyramids   Egypt   ever   to   to   been   the   have   see   you?

_____ ?

_____

g mother   look   your   you   like   do?

_____ ?

_____

2 **T.3**   Reply to the following sentences with a suitable question.

> **Example**
> 'I'm going shopping.'
> *What are you going to buy?*

a 'David speaks four languages.'

_____ ?

b 'We had a wonderful meal in that restaurant.'

_____ ?

c 'Joy and Eric paid a lot of money for their house.'

_____ ?

d 'Bob's cat has just had kittens.'

_____ ?

e 'Lily's going to the cinema tonight.'

_____ ?

f 'Joan's writing a letter.'

_____ ?

g 'My job's really interesting.'

_____ ?

h 'We had a wonderful holiday.'

_____ ?

6 Negatives and short answers

1 **T.4**   Complete the sentences with the correct auxiliary in the positive or negative.

> **Examples**
> Anna likes ice-cream but John *doesn't*.
> I don't like ice-cream but Jill *does*.

a I've been to Australia but Anna _____ .

b Maria isn't studying hard but I _____ .

c John loves flying but we _____ .

d I watched TV last night but my sister _____ .

e Bill hasn't finished his work but we _____ .

f We don't want to leave early but they _____ .

g They didn't remember my birthday but you _____ .

h Your English is really improving but mine _____ .

2 Answer the questions about you with a short answer and some more information.

> **Example**
> Do you speak three languages?
> *Yes, I do. I speak French, German, and Russian.*
> *No, I don't. I only speak two, French and Russian.*

a Are you having a holiday soon?

_____ .

b Did you have a good holiday last year?

_____ .

c Have you ever been to Amsterdam?

_____ .

d Do you often travel abroad?

_____ .

e Does your best friend sometimes go on holiday with you?

_____ .

have/have got

⚠️

1. *Have* and *have got* are both used for possession. *Have got* refers to the present and to all time, even though it looks like the Present Perfect.
   I've got two sisters. I have two sisters.
   She has blond hair. She's got blond hair.

2. There are two forms for the question, the negative, and the short answer.
   Have *you* **got** *any money?* *Yes, I* **have.**
   Do *you* **have** *any money?* *Yes, I* **do.**

   He **hasn't got** *a dog.*
   He **doesn't have** *a dog.*

3. In all other tenses and verb forms, we use *have*, not *have got*.
   I **had** *a bike when I was ten.*
   I **didn't have** *a car until I was twenty-five.*
   I've **had** *a headache all morning.*
   I'll **have** *a steak, please.*
   I love **having** *a dog.*
   I'd like **to have** *another dog.*

4. *Have*, not *have got*, is used for many actions and experiences.
   have breakfast/a cup of tea/a cigarette/
       a break/dinner
   have a bath/a shower/a shave/a rest
   have a swim/a good time/a party/a holiday
   have a chat/a row/a bad dream
   have a look at something/a word with someone

5. *Have got* is more informal. We use it more in spoken English. We use *have* more in written English.
   Have with the *do/does* forms is more common in American English.

7 Sentence completion

T.5 Complete the sentences with the correct form of *have* or *have got*. There are questions, negatives, positives, and various tenses.

Example
Excuse me! *Do you have* the time, please?
or
Excuse me! *Have you got* the time, please?

a I'm starving. I _____ anything to eat last night.

b 'Excuse me! _____ a light, please?'

   'Sorry. I don't smoke.'

c 'Why's Ann taking some aspirin?'

   'Because she _____ a headache.'

d 'What would you like to drink?'

   'I _____ a Coke, please.'

e 'Can you lend me two pounds?'

   'Sorry. I _____ _____ any money on me at all.'

f Maria _____ her baby. It's a girl. They're calling her Lily.

g We _____ a party next Saturday. Would you like to come?

h David! Can I _____ a word with you for a moment?

i How was the party last night? _____ you _____ a good time?

j Peter, could you help me? I _____ a problem, and I don't know what to do.

k 'What time _____ she usually _____ lunch?'

   'About 1.00.'

Vocabulary

8 Holidays and medicine

1 In the text about the Wonders of the Modern World in the Student's Book, the journalist mentioned holidays and medicine. Complete this vocabulary network on holidays with words from the box. Some are done to help you.

water-skiing	traveller's cheques	youth hostel
rucksack	flight attendant	camp-site
caravan	swimming costume	~~suitcase~~
~~hotel~~	farmhouse	relaxing
exploring	beach towel	sight-seeing
ski instructor	guest-house	tour guide
travel agent	sunbathing	suntan lotion

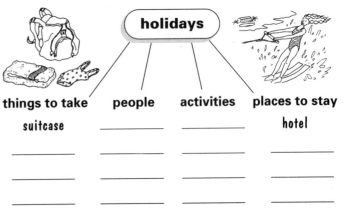

things to take   **people**   **activities**   **places to stay**

suitcase   _____   _____   hotel

_____   _____   _____   _____

_____   _____   _____   _____

_____   _____   _____   _____

_____   _____

2 In the box are words to do with medicine. They can be divided into four groups. Decide what the four groups are, then complete the network.

surgeon	heart	stomach	injection	lungs
sore throat	patient	X-ray	prescription	cough
constipation	rash	specialist	operation	liver
diarrhoea	kidney	sprain	check-up	pills

medicine

things that doctors give you

9 Phonetic script

1 **T.6** Look at the phonetic transcription and write the words next to them. They are all words from Unit 1. There is a list of phonetic symbols on the inside cover of this book.

a /ˈbrekfəst/ _____

b /kəmˈpjuːtə/ _____

c /ˈnɒlɪdʒ/ _____

d /ˈhʌŋgri/ _____

e /ɜːθ/ _____

f /ˈnjuːzpeɪpə/ _____

g /ˌmjuːzɪkl ˈɪnstrəmənt/ _____

h /trəˈdɪʃn/ _____

i /ˈdʒɜːnəlɪst/ _____

j /ˈwepənz/ _____

k /ˈstætʃuː/ _____

2 **T.7** Read the poem and transcribe the words in phonetic script to complete the lines. Read the poem aloud to yourself to practise the pronunciation.

I WONDER

a   I wonder why /ðə grɑːs ɪz griːn/,
b   And why /ðə wɪnd ɪz nevə siːn/.

c   Who taught /ðə bɜːdz tə bɪld ə nest/,
d   And told /ðə triːz tə teɪk ə rest/?

e   And when /ðə muːn ɪz nɒt kwaɪt raʊnd/,
f   Where can /ðə mɪsɪŋ bɪt bi faʊnd/?

g Who /laɪts ðə stɑːz/, when they blow out,
h   And /meɪks ðə laɪtnɪŋ/ flash about?

i   Who paints /ðə reɪnbəʊ ɪn ðə skaɪ/,
j   And hangs /ðə flʌfi klaʊdz səʊ haɪ/?

Why is it now, do you suppose,
That Dad won't tell me if he knows?

Jeannie Kirby

a _____

b _____

c _____

d _____

e _____

f _____

g _____

h _____

i _____

j _____

Prepositions

10 Verb + preposition

Many verbs are followed by a particular preposition. Fill each gap with a preposition from the box. Some are used more than once.

of	about	to	in	with	for	on

a I think you're wrong. I don't agree _____ you at all.

b I'm not interested _____ what you think or what you want.

c We might have a picnic. It depends _____ the weather.

d What are you listening _____ ?

e If you have a problem, talk _____ the teacher.

f 'What did you talk _____ ?'
  'Oh, this and that.'

g You aren't concentrating on your work. What are you thinking

  _____ ?

h 'What do you think _____ Pete?'
  'I really like him.'

i Where's the cash desk? I'd like to pay _____ this book.

j 'I've lost your pen. Sorry ...'
  'It's all right. Don't worry _____ it.'

Grammar words

11 Terminology

It helps to know some of the words used to talk about grammar.
Match a term and its abbreviation from **B** with an example in **A**.

A	B
a write, want	preposition (*prep*)
b she, him	adjective (*adj*)
c car, tree	adverb (*adv*)
d can, must	modal auxiliary verb
e slowly, always	pronoun (*pron*)
f nice, pretty	full verb
g bigger, older	countable noun (C)
h to like	uncountable noun (U)
i a	comparative adjective (*comp adj*)
j on, at, under	superlative adjective (*superl adj*)
k hoping, living	infinitive with *to* (*infin* with *to*)
l the	-*ing* form of the verb (-*ing* form)
m fastest, hottest	past participle (*pp*)
n done, broken	definite article (*def art*)
o rice, weather	indefinite article (*indef art*)

Present time
always

1 Profiles

Read the profiles of the different people.

Which paragraphs go with who?

Put them in the right order.

Vichai is 18. He lives in a townhouse with his family in Bangkok, Thailand.

Sue Morris and her husband Geoff run a corner shop in North Carlton, a suburb of Melbourne, Australia. This kind of shop is called a milkbar.

13-year-old Ursula Buhlmann lives with her family in Lucerne, Switzerland.

a **His older sister** also lives at home. Their house is near Kasertsart University, where he is in the second year of an engineering course. Lessons start at 8 in the morning and go on until 3 in the afternoon, Monday till Friday. When he graduates, he wants to be a civil engineer.

b '**My father** is a lorry driver and my mother is a housewife. I'm the youngest of five children. We live in a small block of flats with five other families in the old part of town.'

c 'I usually have boiled rice for breakfast, then at lunch-time I have chicken with fried rice or a bowl of noodles in the university canteen. In the evening I eat with my family. My mother cooks. Her food's the best in the whole world!'

d 'Shops like these are like community meeting places. We look after people's keys, pass on messages, look after kids, we even cash cheques for those people who never have time to go to the bank.'

e It takes her about fifteen minutes to walk to school, but in summer she goes by bike. She's in the second year of the Mariahilf secondary school. It has about 250 pupils, with eighteen to twenty girls and boys in each class.

f At the weekend he earns some extra money teaching computer studies at a private computer school. He enjoys playing 'takraw', a Thai game played with a light ball made of rattan, which you can hit with your foot, knee, elbow or heel, but not your hand. He loves living in Bangkok, but he hates the traffic and traffic jams, which get worse every year.

g 'I have about thirty lessons a week from Monday to Saturday, starting at 7.45 am and going on until 4.30 or 5.00 pm, with Wednesday and Saturday afternoons free and a lunch-break of two and a half hours every day. Schools here don't provide lunch so everyone goes home. When I leave school, I want to work with children, maybe in a kindergarten.'

h **It sells** all sorts of food and household goods from sandwiches to washing-up liquid, from magazines to nails and screws. 'We offer a huge range of products. It's like three or four shops rolled into one.'

i The hours are terribly long. The shop opens at 6.00 am and closes at 10.00 pm, except on Sunday when it's 8.30 am until 9.30 pm. Their whole lives are controlled by the shop. 'There are a lot of things we can't do anymore. We don't go to the movies, we don't go camping at the weekend. But it's the long hours that make the money.'

2 Sentence completion

Complete the sentences about the people in Exercise 1.

a Sue and Geoff _____ a shop.

b This kind of shop _____ a milkbar.

c Most days the shop _____ at 10.00 pm.

d They _____ camping any more.

e Ursula _____ four brothers and sisters.

f It _____ her fifteen minutes _____ to school.

g She _____ school at 7.45 am.

h Her school _____ lunch.

i 'When I _____ , I _____ to be a civil engineer.'

j 'I _____ lunch in the university canteen.'

k 'I _____ extra money teaching computer studies.'

l 'I _____ the traffic in Bangkok.'

3 Questions

T.8   Here are the answers to some questions about the Profiles in Exercise 1. Write the questions.

a _____ ?
All sorts of food and household goods.

b _____ ?
Six am.

c Why _____ movies _____ ?
Because they work such long hours.

d _____ ?
He's a lorry driver.

e _____ ?
In a small block of flats.

f _____ ?
Eighteen to twenty.

g _____ ?
About thirty a week.

h _____ ?
Two and a half hours.

i _____ ?
She wants to work with children.

j Who_____ live _____ ?
With his parents and his sister.

k _____ ?
Boiled rice.

l _____ ?
Takraw.

m _____ ?
Yes, he loves it, but he hates the traffic.

4 Negatives

Complete the sentences with a negative.

a Vegetarians _____ .

b A vegan _____ .

c An atheist _____ .

d I'm unemployed. I _____ .

e My father's bald. He _____ .

f They are penniless. They _____ .

g Selfish people _____ other people.

Pronunciation

5 -s at the end of a word

T.9   Remember the rules for the pronunciation of -s at the end of a word. This applies to the third person singular in the Present Simple and to plural nouns.

1 If the word ends in ... /s/, /z/, /ʃ/, /tʃ/, or /dʒ/
   ... the final -s is pronounced /ɪz/.

misses	*buses*	*chooses*	*sizes*
washes	*dishes*	*watches*	*matches*
manages	*badges*		

2 If the word ends in ... /p/, /t/, /k/, /f/, or /θ/
   ... the final -s is pronounced /s/.

stops	*ships*	*hits*	*pets*
attacks	*bricks*	*laughs*	*coughs*
maths			

3 If the word ends in ... /b/, /d/, /g/, /v/, /ð/, /l/, /m/, /n/, /ŋ/, or any vowel sound
   ... the final -s is pronounced /z/.

stabs	*cabs*	*leads*	*hands*
begs	*bags*	*leaves*	*waves*
breathes	*rolls*	*hills*	*hums*
trams	*earns*	*cans*	*sings*
goes	*news*	*hires*	*fears*
wears	*chairs*	*songs*	

T.10 The words in the box all appeared in the Profiles in Exercise 1. Put them in the right column according to the pronunciation of -s at the end of the word.

girls	boys	cheques	places	lives
hours	earns	products	loves	minutes
shops	closes	graduates	lessons	wants
kids	keys	messages	schools	
hates	cooks	sandwiches	things	

/ɪz/ (4 words)	/s/ (8 words)	/z/ (11 words)

Present states and actions

6 Present Simple and Present Continuous

1 **T.11** Look at the pictures and read about Liam, who is an actor.

Liam, actor

Workday Liam is an actor. He sometimes makes films and sometimes works in the theatre. He often acts in Shakespearean plays and wears beautiful costumes. He doesn't earn a lot of money because he isn't very well-known.

Now At the moment he isn't working, he's relaxing at home. He's wearing jeans and a T-shirt and drinking coffee. He's waiting for the phone to ring because he needs more work.

2 Write about these people in the same way.

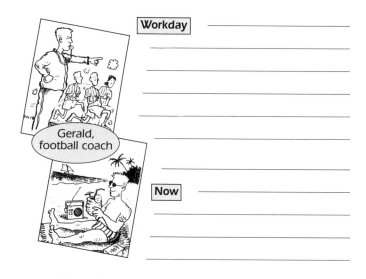

Rita, traffic warden

Workday _____

Now _____

Gerald, football coach

Workday _____

Now _____

Tony and Peggy, organic farmers

Workday _____

Now _____

7 Present Simple or Present Continuous?

1 Some sentences are right and some are wrong. Put a (✔) next to the right ones and a cross (✘) next to the wrong ones. Correct the wrong sentences.

a ☐ I'm thinking you are very impolite.

b ☐ Where are you thinking of going on holiday?

c ☐ Why do you leave so early? Don't you enjoy the party?

d ☐ Nobody is ever laughing at my husband's jokes. It's so embarrassing.

e ☐ I don't believe a word he says. He always tells lies.

f ☐ We're seeing our son's teacher at four o'clock.

g ☐ I'm not seeing what your problem is.

h ☐ Does the newsagent sell stamps?

i ☐ He's never knowing the answer.

2 **T.12** Put the verbs in the correct form, Present Simple or Present Continuous.

Conversation 1

A What (a) _____ (you/do)?

B I (b) _____ (pack) my suitcase. I

(c) _____ (leave) you and this house.

A But I (d) _____ (not/understand).

Where (e) _____ (you/go)?

B I (f) _____ (not/know). The only

thing I (g) _____ (know) is that Peter

(h) _____ (meet) me at
the airport at six o'clock.

Conversation 2

A What (a) _____ (that man/do)
over there?

B He (b) _____ (wait) for the bank to open.

A But the banks (c) _____ (not open)
on Saturday afternoons.

B (d) _____ (you/think) he's a bank robber?

Watch out! He (e) _____
(take) something out of his pocket. He

(f) _____ (walk) towards us!

C Excuse me. Could you tell me the time, please?

3 Complete the pairs of sentences with the verb in *italics*. Use the Present Simple for one and the Present Continuous for the other.

a *think*

I _____ of learning how to fly a plane.

I _____ that's a good idea.

b *see*

_____ you _____ what I mean?

What time _____ you _____
the bank manager?

c *have*

She _____ a wonderful suntan.

She _____ a wonderful time in Spain.

8 *always*

⚠

1 *Always* is usually used with the Present Simple, like other adverbs of frequency.

> I **always** drive to work.
> He **sometimes** helps me with my homework.
> We **never** drink beer.

2 *Always* can also be used with the Present Continuous, but there is a change in meaning.

> She **always** has a shower after work.
> = She does this every time.
> She's **always** having showers.
> = She does this too often.
> You **always** drink beer.
> = You do this every time (we go to the pub).
> You're **always** drinking beer.
> = You do this too often. You drink too much.
> He **always** buys me flowers.
> = He does this every time (when it's my birthday).
> He's **always** buying me flowers.
> = He does this more than is usual (not just for my birthday).

3 *Always* + Present Continuous is often used to suggest criticism in the opinion of the speaker.

> You're **always** complaining about something!
> She's **always** going shopping!
> I'm **always** losing my glasses!

T.13 Complete the conversations using *always* + Present Simple or Present Continuous. Choose which is more appropriate.

a **A** I've left my homework at home again.
   B I don't believe it! You …

b **A** We're going on holiday to Spain next week.
   B How lovely! You went to Spain last year, didn't you?
   A Yes, we did. We …

c **A** Bob and Janet are going on holiday next week.
   B What? Again? They …

d **A** I've just spent £2,000 on new clothes. I've bought four pairs of shoes and three new suits.
   B How can you afford it? You …

e **A** I always walk to work.
   B I don't. It's too far to walk. I …

f **A** My car's old but it never breaks down.
   B You're lucky. My car's not as old as yours and it …

Present passive

9 Past participles

Add the past participle to the following sentences. Choose from the verbs in the box. Use each verb once only.

grow	produce	make	pull down	take
deliver	include	employ	decorate	speak

a English is _____ here.

b Volvos are _____ in Sweden.

c Is service _____ in the bill?

d Our kitchen is being _____ at the moment.

e Whisky is _____ in Scotland.

f Our factory is being _____ over by an American company.

g About one thousand people are _____ in that factory.

h Lots of tulips are _____ in Holland.

i That block of flats is being _____ because it is unsafe.

j In Britain milk is _____ to your doorstep.

10 Active or passive?

T.14 Look at the text on *Catching a plane*. Put the verb in the correct form, Present Simple active or Present Simple passive.

Catching a plane

When you **(a)** _____ (arrive) at an airport, you should go straight to the check-in desk where your ticket and luggage **(b)** _____ (check).

You **(c)** _____ (keep) your hand luggage with you but your suitcases **(d)** _____ (take) to the plane on a conveyor belt. You can now go to the departure lounge.

If you are on an international flight, your passport **(e)** _____ (check), and then you and your bags **(f)** _____ (x-ray) by security cameras; sometimes you **(g)** _____ (give) a body search and your luggage **(h)** _____ (search) by a security officer. You **(i)** _____ (wait) in the departure lounge until your flight **(j)** _____ (call) and you **(k)** _____ (tell) which number gate to go to.

Finally you **(l)** _____ (board) your plane and you **(m)** _____ (show) to your seat by a flight attendant.

11 A poem

1 **T.15** Read the poem. Use your dictionary.

A MAN IS MADE

A man is made
Of flesh and blood
Of eyes and bones and water.
The very same things make his son
As those that make
His daughter.

A tree is made
Of leaf and sap,
Of bark and fruit and berries.
It keeps a bird's nest
In its boughs
And blackbirds eat the cherries.

A table's made
Of naked wood
Planed smooth as milk. I wonder
If tables ever dream of sun,
Of wind, and rain, and thunder?

And when man takes
His axe and strikes
And sets the sawdust flying –
Is it a table being born?
Or just a tree that's dying?

2 Find examples of present active and passive forms.

3 Read the poem aloud and/or learn it by heart!

Vocabulary

12 Synonyms and antonyms

We often use prefixes to form the opposite of an adjective. The most common prefixes are *un-*, *in-*, *im-*. Complete the columns. Write one opposite adjective using a prefix, and another opposite adjective which is a different word from the box.

~~sad~~	out of date	stupid	ugly	arrogant	cheap
cruel	strange/rare	casual	rude	boring	wrong

Adjective	Opposite (Adj + prefix)	Opposite (different word)
happy	*unhappy*	*sad*
polite		
expensive		
interesting		
correct		
attractive		
fashionable		
intelligent		
usual		
kind		
formal		
modest		

Multi-word verbs

13 *look* and *be*

1 Look at the dictionary extracts of some multi-word verbs with *look*.

look forward to sth/doing to wait with pleasure for sth to happen: *We're really looking forward to our holiday.* **look out** to be careful or to pay attention to sth dangerous, etc: *Look out! There's a car coming!* **look sth up** to search for information in a book: *to look up the times for trains to London.*

Complete the sentences using a multi-word verb with *look*.

Example
Babysitters *look after children* while their parents go out.

a If I don't know the meaning of a word, I

_____ it _____ in the dictionary.

b I'm _____ my glasses. Have you seen them anywhere?

c Look _____ ! That glass is going to fall!

d (Ending a letter) I _____ to hearing from you soon.

e Look _____ that strange man over there! What's he doing?

f The nurses _____ my grandmother very well when she was in hospital.

2 The verb *to be* is often followed by a particle to form a multi-word verb.

Example
*Goodbye! **I'm off** to Australia for three weeks.*
(= I'm going …)

Put a word from the box into each gap. Some are used more than once.

on	up	in	up to	off	away

a (On the telephone in an office)
'Hello. Can I speak to Mr James, please?'
'I'm sorry. He isn't _____ at the moment. Can I take a message?'

b 'Hello. Can I speak to Mr James, please?'
'I'm sorry. He's _____ on holiday at the moment. Can I help you?'

c 'I feel like going to the cinema tonight.'
'Good idea! What's _____ at the moment?'

d I think this milk's _____ . It smells horrid.

e 'Where shall we go for a meal?'
'It's _____ you. It's your birthday. *You* choose.'

f Come on, kids! Aren't you _____ yet? Breakfast's on the table.

g I wonder why they aren't answering the door. There must be someone _____ . All the lights are _____ .

h I must be _____ soon. I want to get to the shops before they close.

i 'Why isn't there any hot water?'
'The central heating's _____ . That's why.'

j 'You're crying. What's _____ ?'
'I'm just a bit sad. That's all.'

Past time
while, during and *for*

Past Simple and Past Continuous

1 A sad story

1 Look at the pictures. They tell the unfortunate story of Mrs Maisie Taylor and her cat, Billy.

The verbs and phrases opposite tell the events of the story but they are not in the right order. Put the correct picture number into the boxes.

Past Simple	Past Continuous
☐ ran up	☐ was waiting
☐ killed	☐ was watering the plants
☐ arrived	☐ were leaving
☐ put up	☐ was playing
☐ called	☐ were having tea
☐ rang	
☐ rescued	
☐ ran him over	
☐ couldn't get down	
☐ invited them for tea	
☐ tried to tempt him down	

2 **T.16** Complete the story about Mrs Taylor using the correct verbs and phrases from the boxes.

Yesterday evening, Mrs Taylor **(a)** _____

_____ in her garden, while her cat,

Billy, **(b)** _____ near her. Suddenly, Billy

(c) _____ a tree. Mrs Taylor **(d)** _____ to

Billy, but he **(e)** _____ , so she

(f) _____ the Fire Brigade. While she

(g) _____ for them to arrive, she

(h) _____ with some fish.

The Fire Brigade eventually **(i)** _____ ,

(j) _____ their ladder and **(k)** _____

Billy. Mrs Taylor was so pleased that she

(l) _____ . While they

(m) _____ , they didn't see Billy go

outside again, and ten minutes later, as they

(n) _____ , they **(o)** _____

and unfortunately they **(p)** _____ him.

2 Correcting facts

The following statements about the story are *all* incorrect. Correct each one first with a negative statement and then add the correct information.

Example
The story happened last month.
The story didn't happen last month, it happened yesterday evening.

a Mrs Taylor was cutting the grass.

_____

_____

b Billy was sleeping in the garden.

_____

_____

c Billy jumped over the wall.

_____

_____

d Mrs Taylor rang the Police.

_____

_____

e The Fire Brigade used a rope to get Billy down.

_____

_____

f Billy died when he fell from the tree.

_____

_____

3 Past Simple or Past Continuous?

Underline the correct verb form.

Example
We *met*/were meeting when we lived/*were living* in Italy.

a She *worked/was working* quietly at her desk when suddenly the door *opened/was opening* and her daughter *rushed/was rushing* in.

b He *stood/was standing* up, *walked/was walking* across the room, and *closed/was closing* the window.

c A strange man *walked/was walking* into the room. He *wore/was wearing* red trousers and a pink shirt.

d *Didn't you meet/Weren't you meeting* your wife while you *worked/were working* in Chile?

e I *saw/was seeing* you in the park yesterday. You *sat/were sitting* on a bench with your arm round Tom.

f As soon as I *walked/was walking* into the room, he *handed/was handing* me the letter.

g His father was really angry with him because he *listened/was listening* to music while he *did/was doing* his homework.

h Why *didn't they visit/weren't they visiting* me while they *stayed/were staying* in London?

i As he *passed/was passing* the bank, a man in a mask *knocked/was knocking* him onto the ground.

j What *did you write/were you writing* when your computer *crashed/was crashing*?

4 A holiday in Madeira

T.17 Put the verbs in brackets into the correct form, Past Simple or Past Continuous.

A special holiday in Madeira

Last February, I (**a**) _____ (decide) to go on holiday to the island of Madeira. On the morning I (**b**) _____ (leave) England it (**c**) _____ (rain), but when I (**d**) _____ (land) in Funchal, the capital of Madeira, the sun (**e**) _____ (shine) and a lovely, warm breeze (**f**) _____ (blow) from the sea. I (**g**) _____ (take) a taxi to my hotel. As I (**h**) _____ (sign) the register, someone (**i**) _____ (tap) me on the shoulder. I (**j**) _____ (not can) believe my eyes! It was my old girlfriend. She (**k**) _____ (stay) at the same hotel. The next day, we (**l**) _____ (go) for a walk together in the hills and we (**m**) _____ (see) hundreds of beautiful wild flowers. It (**n**) _____ (get) dark when we (**o**) _____ (return) to our hotel after a very interesting day. We (**p**) _____ (spend) the rest of the week together; it was very romantic. We (**q**) _____ (feel) very sad when the holiday (**r**) _____ (end).

5 What did he do? What was he doing?

Read the stories and answer the questions.

Hero saves man's life

Thirty-eight-year-old Jack Easton was driving home from work at around 6.30 in the evening when he saw a yellow VW van, driven by Ken Sharpe, crash into a tree. Without thinking of his own safety, he pulled the young man out of the van and took him straight to hospital. Ken is making good progress.

Lottery win for unemployed man

Unemployed painter, John Parrott, received a very pleasant surprise last night. He was at home repairing his car when a man from the lottery came to his house to inform him that he had won £300,000. He immediately gave his wife a big kiss and took his whole family out for a slap-up meal.

SHOCK FOR BANK CUSTOMERS

Customers in BARCLAYS BANK, Heston, received a terrible shock yesterday. People were standing in queues chatting to each other when two masked robbers burst into the bank. 60-year-old Martin Webb suffered a heart attack and was taken to hospital. The robbers escaped with £500.

a What was Jack doing when he saw the accident?

_____

_____

_____

b What did Jack do when he saw the accident?

_____

_____

_____

c What was John Parrott doing when he heard the good news?

_____

_____

_____

d What did John Parrott do when he heard the good news?

_____

_____

_____

e What was happening in the bank when the robbers burst in?

_____

_____

_____

f What happened to Martin Webb when the robbers burst in?

_____

_____

_____

Past Perfect

6 Regular and irregular verbs

Complete the chart with the missing verb forms.

Infinitive	Past Simple	Past participle
grow		
	left	
		fallen
find		
		sold
feel		
		driven
fly		
	left	
travel		
lie (not tell the truth)		
		won
	spent	

7 Choosing the right tense

<u>Underline</u> the correct tense in the story.

It was ten o'clock in the evening. Peter (**a**) *sat/had sat* down on his sofa and thought about the day. What a busy day it (**b**) *was!/had been!* This was his first night in his own flat. He (**c**) *lived/had lived* his entire life in the family home, and now for the first time, he (**d**) *was/had been* on his own.

He sat surrounded by boxes that they (**e**) *didn't manage/hadn't managed* to unpack during the day. It (**f**) *took/had taken* months to get all his things together. His mother (**g**) *was/had been* very generous, buying him things like towels and mugs.

He (**h**) *went/had gone* into the kitchen and (**i**) *got/had got* a beer from the fridge. He suddenly (**j**) *felt/had felt* very tired and yawned. No wonder he (**k**) *was/had been tired*! He (**l**) *was/had been* up since six o'clock in the morning. He (**m**) *decided/had decided* to finish his beer and go to bed.

8 Sentence completion

T.18 Complete the sentences, or add a sentence, using the ideas in brackets and a verb in the Past Perfect.

Example
I was broke because I … (spend/money/clothes)
I was broke because I had spent all my money on clothes.

a Jane was furious … (oversleep and miss the bus)

_____

_____

b Mary was very disappointed with her son. She … (send/good school; but he /not do any work; fail/exams)

_____

_____

c Brian was sent to prison for three years. He … (steal money/employer; spend/drugs)

_____

_____

d I was very nervous as I waited in the departure lounge. I … (never/fly/before)

_____

_____

e Jack wanted a new challenge in his work. He … (be/same job/ten years)

_____

_____

f I didn't know his name, but the face was familiar. I was sure … (see/somewhere/before)

_____

_____

g Mick was now a penniless beggar, but he … (not always/be/poor. be/millionaire; business/ collapse; lose/everything)

_____

_____

h When I got home, I was starving. I … (not have/ anything to eat all day)

_____

_____

9 *had* or *would*?

Say if *'d* is the contracted form of *had* or *would*.

Examples
I'd like a cup of tea. = *would*
I knew I'd seen him before. = *had*

a You must try bunjee jumping! You'd love it!
b She said she'd give him everything.
c She said she'd given him everything.
d I was tired because I'd been up since six.
e I told you they'd arrive on time!
f I told you they'd bought the house!

Past Simple active and passive

10 Biographies

T.19 Look at the photographs and read the biographies of three brave people. Fill the gaps with the correct verb.

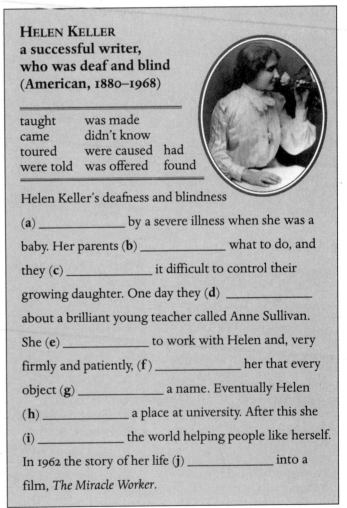

HELEN KELLER
**a successful writer,
who was deaf and blind**
(American, 1880–1968)

taught	was made	
came	didn't know	
toured	were caused	had
were told	was offered	found

Helen Keller's deafness and blindness

(**a**) _____ by a severe illness when she was a baby. Her parents (**b**) _____ what to do, and they (**c**) _____ it difficult to control their growing daughter. One day they (**d**) _____ about a brilliant young teacher called Anne Sullivan. She (**e**) _____ to work with Helen and, very firmly and patiently, (**f**) _____ her that every object (**g**) _____ a name. Eventually Helen (**h**) _____ a place at university. After this she (**i**) _____ the world helping people like herself. In 1962 the story of her life (**j**) _____ into a film, *The Miracle Worker*.

**CHARLES BLONDIN
the world's most famous
tightrope walker
(French, 1824–1897)**

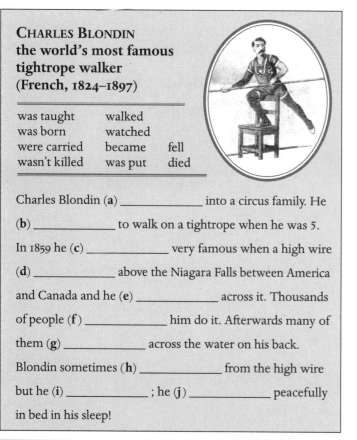

was taught	walked	
was born	watched	
were carried	became	fell
wasn't killed	was put	died

Charles Blondin (**a**) _____ into a circus family. He

(**b**) _____ to walk on a tightrope when he was 5.

In 1859 he (**c**) _____ very famous when a high wire

(**d**) _____ above the Niagara Falls between America

and Canada and he (**e**) _____ across it. Thousands

of people (**f**) _____ him do it. Afterwards many of

them (**g**) _____ across the water on his back.

Blondin sometimes (**h**) _____ from the high wire

but he (**i**) _____ ; he (**j**) _____ peacefully

in bed in his sleep!

**AMY JOHNSON
the first woman pilot
to fly to Australia
(English, 1903–1941)**

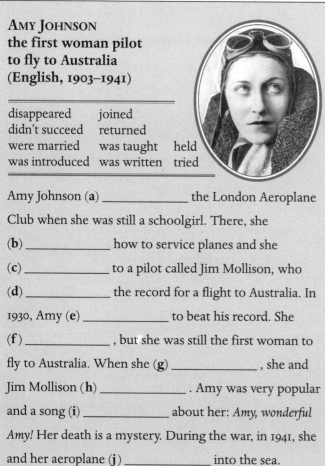

disappeared	joined	
didn't succeed	returned	
were married	was taught	held
was introduced	was written	tried

Amy Johnson (**a**) _____ the London Aeroplane

Club when she was still a schoolgirl. There, she

(**b**) _____ how to service planes and she

(**c**) _____ to a pilot called Jim Mollison, who

(**d**) _____ the record for a flight to Australia. In

1930, Amy (**e**) _____ to beat his record. She

(**f**) _____ , but she was still the first woman to

fly to Australia. When she (**g**) _____ , she and

Jim Mollison (**h**) _____ . Amy was very popular

and a song (**i**) _____ about her: *Amy, wonderful

Amy!* Her death is a mystery. During the war, in 1941, she

and her aeroplane (**j**) _____ into the sea.

11 *Somebody did that!*

Rewrite the sentences using the passive.

Examples
Somebody stole my handbag.
My handbag was stolen.
Nobody asked him to come.
He wasn't asked to come.

a Somebody robbed the bank last night.

The bank_____

b Somebody told me to wait outside.

I_____

c Nobody invited her to the party.

She _____

d Somebody drove them to the airport.

They_____

e Nobody sent us any tickets.

We _____

f Did anybody find the missing child?

Was _____ ?

g Did anything disturb you in the night?

Were _____ ?

while, during and *for*

⚠️

1 *While* is a conjunction, and is followed by a clause.

> ***While** I was getting ready, I listened to the radio.
> I met my wife **while** I was at university.*

2 *During* is a preposition, and is followed by a noun.
It tells us *when* something happened. It means
at some point in a period of time.

> *We had to call a doctor **during** the night.
> Can I speak to you **during** the break?*

We cannot use *during* with a period of time.

> **We talked ~~during five minutes~~.
> *We're on holiday ~~during six weeks~~.*

3 *For* is a preposition, and is followed by a noun.
It tells us *how long* something lasts.

> *We talked **for** five minutes.
> We're going on holiday **for** six weeks.*

12 Gap filling

Put *while*, *during*, or *for* into each gap.

a My uncle died _____ the war.

b The phone rang _____ I was having supper.

c I lived in Paris _____ several years.

d _____ I was in Paris I made a lot of friends.

e I was in hospital _____ three weeks.

f _____ my stay in hospital, the nurses looked after me very well.

g A football match lasts _____ ninety minutes.

h I hurt my leg _____ I was playing football yesterday.

i I hurt my leg _____ the second half of the match.

j Traffic is always bad _____ the rush hour.

k Last week I was held up _____ three hours.

l Peter came round _____ we were eating.

m Peter came round _____ the meal.

Vocabulary

13 Adverbs

T.20 Put the adverb on the right in the correct place in the sentence. Sometimes more than one place is possible.

Example

The film was good.   *quite*

I phoned the police.   *immediately*

a I got up late this morning, but I managed to catch the bus.   *just* *fortunately*

b 'Hi, Pete. How are you?'
'My name's John, but don't worry.'   *actually*

c In the middle of the picnic it began to rain.   *suddenly*

d I saw Mary at the party. I didn't see anyone else.   *only*

e I gave a present to John, not to anyone else.   *only*

f Jane and I have been friends. We went to school. We were born in the same hospital.   *even* *together* *always*

g 'You know I applied for that job.'
'Which job?'
'The one based in Paris.'
'No. I don't know anything about it.'
'I didn't get it.'   *anyway*

h 'I didn't like it.'
'I didn't like it.'   *either*

i 'I like it.'
'I like it.'   *too*

Here are three more sentences which don't make sense without the adverbs.

j Everybody in our family loves ice-cream, me.   *really* *especially*

k The traffic to the airport was bad that we missed the plane.   *nearly* *so*

l I'm tall to be a policeman, but I haven't got qualifications.   *enough* *enough*

Prepositions

14 in, at, on for time

> **1** We use *at* for times and certain expressions.
>
> | | |
> |---|---|
> | **at** *8.00* | **at** *midnight* |
> | **at** *lunchtime* | **at** *the weekend* |
> | **at** *Christmas* | **at** *the same time* |
> | **at** *the moment* | **at** *the age of 9* |
>
> **2** We use *on* for days and dates.
>
> | | |
> |---|---|
> | **on** *Friday* | **on** *Friday morning* |
> | **on** *12 September* | **on** *Saturday evening* |
>
> **3** We use *in* for longer periods such as months, years, and seasons.
>
> | | |
> |---|---|
> | **in** *April* | **in** *1965* |
> | **in** *summer* | **in** *the nineteenth century* |
>
> We say, *at night* but *in the evening/afternoon*.
> We also say, *I'll see you in the morning*,
> but *I'll see you tomorrow morning*.
>
> **4** There is no preposition before *last*, *next*, or *this*.
> What did you do **last night**?
> I'll see you **next week**.

Put *in*, *at*, *on*, or nothing into each gap.

a 'It's my birthday ____ next week.'

  'When?'

  '____ Monday.'

  '____ what time were you born?'

  '____ 8.00 ____ the morning.'

b 'I'm meeting Alan ____ this evening.'

  'What time?'

  '____ six.'

c 'What did you do ____ the weekend?'

  '____ Friday evening we went to a party. We slept in late ____ Saturday morning, and then ____ the afternoon we went shopping. ____ 7.00 some friends came round for a drink. We didn't do anything ____ Sunday. What about you?'

d The weather in England is unreliable. ____ summer it can be hot, but it often rains ____ April and June. ____ last year the summer was awful. The best English weather is ____ spring and autumn.

e I learned to drive ____ 1980 ____ the age of 17. My brother learned ____ the same time as me, but I passed first.

f I'll phone you ____ next week. ____ Thursday, maybe. ____ the afternoon. ____ about 3.00. OK?

g I don't see my parents much. ____ Christmas, usually, and ____ the holidays.

Pronunciation

15 Words that sound the same

T.21   In each sentence there are two words in phonetic script. They have the *same* pronunciation but *different* meanings and spellings. Write in the words.

Example
The Queen was /θrəʊn/ *thrown* off the /θrəʊn/ *throne* .

a She /θru:/ _____ the ring /θru:/ _____ the window and into the garden.

b The soldiers /wɔ:/ _____ khaki uniforms when they went to /wɔ:/ _____ .

c I must /wɔ:n/ _____ you that ties must be /wɔ:n/ _____ at the Ritz.

d The police /kɔ:t/ _____ the burglar and he ended up in /kɔ:t/ _____ in front of Judge Jordan.

e I /blu:/ _____ up six red balloons and ten /blu:/ _____ ones for the party.

f We /nju:/ _____ that Sue and Jim had bought a /nju:/ _____ car.

g I /sɔ:/ _____ Jack at the doctor's with a /sɔ:/ _____ throat.

h The book I /red/ _____ had a /red/ _____ cover.

i We /rəʊd/ _____ our horses along the narrow /rəʊd/ _____ .

4 Modal verbs of obligation and permission
can and *be able to*

have to/don't have to

1 What do they have to do?

1 Look at the photos and read the statements below. Who is saying the sentences? Write **a**, **b**, or **c** next to each statement.

b The teenager

a The retired man

c The businesswoman

- [ ] 'I have to wear smart suits.'
- [ ] 'I always have to be home before midnight.'
- [ ] 'I often have to travel overseas.'
- [ ] 'My dad usually has to work in the evenings.'
- [ ] 'I don't have to get up at 6.30 am any more.'
- [ ] 'My husband has to take our children to school every morning.'
- [ ] 'My wife has to go to hospital every week.'
- [ ] 'I have to get good results in my exams.'
- [ ] 'My sister doesn't have to help with the housework.'

2 **T.22** Change each statement in Exercise 1 into a question with *Why* and write it above the relevant answer below.

> Example
> 'Why *do you have to wear smart suits?*'
> 'Because I have to meet a lot of important people.'

a 'Why _____ ?'
'Because I work for an international company.'

b 'Why _____ ?'
'Because my parents say that I have to.'

c 'Why _____ ?'
'Because I don't have to catch the 7.32 am train to work.'

d 'Why _____ ?'
'Because he's a teacher and he has to mark homework.'

e 'Why _____ ?'
'Because she has arthritis and she has to have physiotherapy.'

f 'Why _____ ?'
'Because my mum says that she is still too young.'

g 'Why _____ ?'
'Because I start work very early and he doesn't have to be at work until 9.30 am.'

h 'Why _____ ?'
'Because I want to go to Oxford University.'

2 Forms of *have to*

Complete the sentences with a suitable form of *have to*.

> Examples
> I'm *having to* work very hard at the moment because I have an exam next week.
>
> You *won't have to* work hard after your exam. You can have a holiday.

a My father's a customs official so he always

_____ wear a uniform at work, but

my mother's a teacher so she _____ wear one.

b When I was a teenager, we _____ be

home by nine o'clock. But we _____ take as many exams as teenagers nowadays.

c I can't see the small print very well. I think I _____ wear glasses soon.

d Nobody enjoys _____ get up at five o'clock in the morning.

e _____ we _____ have any vaccinations before we go to Barbados?

f _____ your grandmother _____ leave school when she was only fourteen?

g You _____ be a millionaire to shop in Harrods but it helps!

h If I fail my exam, _____ I _____ take it again?

can and allowed to

3 Who says?

1 Who says the following sentences? Where are the people?

Example
You aren't allowed to sit there. Get off the grass!
The park attendant in a park.

a You can't park there. I'll give you a parking ticket.

b I'm sorry sir, but customers aren't allowed in without a tie.

c You're allowed to bring in 250 cigarettes and a bottle of spirits.

d You can't talk in here. People are studying.

e You can take your safety-belt off now and walk around, but you aren't allowed to smoke in the toilets, and you can't use personal computers.

f We're allowed to make one phone call a week, and we can go to the library, but we spend most of the time in our cells.

2 Think of some things that you *can* and *can't do* in the following places.

Example
a church
You aren't allowed to ride a bike in a church.
You can light a candle and say a prayer.

a a hospital

_____

_____

b a museum

_____

_____

c a swimming pool

_____

_____

d a park

_____

_____

4 Dialogues for permission

T.23 Here are two dialogues mixed up. One is between Jack and his daughter, Jill; the other is between Sam, a businessman, and his boss, Anna. Sort them out and put them in the right order.

n	Jill
	Jack
	Jill
	Jack
	Jill
	Jack
	Jill

j	Sam
	Anna
	Sam
	Anna
	Sam
	Anna
	Sam

a But I'm taking Dave to see his girlfriend in hospital!

b Yes, what is it?

c I told you. *I* need it.

d Well, it's not a very convenient time at the moment. We're very busy.

e You know my father is having problems with his legs and he can't walk. Well, he needs to go into hospital next week, and I was wondering if I could have the day off.

f Thanks a lot, dad. I won't be late back.

g Oh, please! He won't be able to go if I don't give him a lift.

h That's very kind. Thank you very much. I'm very grateful.

i No, you can't. *I* need it.

j Anna? Have you got a minute? Can I have a word?

k I know we're busy, but he won't be able to get to the hospital if I don't take him.

l All right. I suppose I can walk. The exercise will do me good.

m Well, if that's the case then you must take him, of course.

n Dad, can I have the car tonight?

5 can and be able to

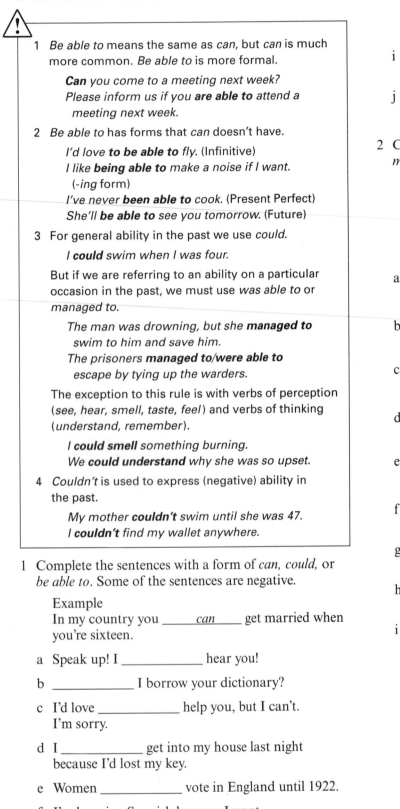

1 *Be able to* means the same as *can*, but *can* is much more common. *Be able to* is more formal.

> **Can** you come to a meeting next week?
> Please inform us if you **are able to** attend a meeting next week.

2 *Be able to* has forms that *can* doesn't have.

> I'd love **to be able to** fly. (Infinitive)
> I like **being able to** make a noise if I want.
> (*-ing* form)
> I've never **been able to** cook. (Present Perfect)
> She'll **be able to** see you tomorrow. (Future)

3 For general ability in the past we use *could*.

> I **could** swim when I was four.

But if we are referring to an ability on a particular occasion in the past, we must use *was able to* or *managed to*.

> The man was drowning, but she **managed to** swim to him and save him.
> The prisoners **managed to/were able to** escape by tying up the warders.

The exception to this rule is with verbs of perception (*see, hear, smell, taste, feel*) and verbs of thinking (*understand, remember*).

> I **could smell** something burning.
> We **could understand** why she was so upset.

4 *Couldn't* is used to express (negative) ability in the past.

> My mother **couldn't** swim until she was 47.
> I **couldn't** find my wallet anywhere.

1 Complete the sentences with a form of *can, could,* or *be able to*. Some of the sentences are negative.

Example
In my country you _____can_____ get married when you're sixteen.

a Speak up! I _____ hear you!

b _____ I borrow your dictionary?

c I'd love _____ help you, but I can't. I'm sorry.

d I _____ get into my house last night because I'd lost my key.

e Women _____ vote in England until 1922.

f I'm learning Spanish because I want _____ speak to people when I'm in Mexico.

g The doctor says I _____ walk again in two weeks' time.

h I asked the teacher if I _____ open the window, but she said I _____ because it would be too noisy.

i I'm sorry, but I _____ come to your party next week.

j I love driving! _____ drive has changed my whole life.

2 Complete the sentences with *could, couldn't,* or *manage to*.

Example
I phoned the plumber because I _could_ smell gas in the kitchen.

We _managed to_ put out the fire by throwing water on it.

a Jane and John saved and saved, and finally they _____ buy the house of their dreams.

b I phoned you yesterday, but I _____ get an answer. Where were you?

c The neighbours were having a row, and I _____ hear every word they said.

d _____ you speak French before you moved to Paris?

e I went for a ten-mile run last Saturday. It nearly killed me! I _____ move on Sunday.

f _____ you _____ find all the things you wanted at the shops?

g The police _____ find the man who had stolen my car. He was sent to prison.

h My grandfather _____ speak four languages.

i When we got to the top of the mountain we _____ see for miles.

must, should and have to

6 must or have to?

Complete the sentences with *must* or *have to*.

Example

a You _____ stay in bed for a few days.

b I _____ stay in bed for a few days.

c I _____ wash my hair tonight.

d I _____ clean all these shoes!

e I _____ sit in this room for three hours!

g I _____ go and see the doctor.

h Sorry. I can't come on Friday. I _____ go to the doctor's at 3.00.

7 Giving advice

T.24 Give advice to people in the following situations. Use *should*.

a My twenty-year-old son just stays at home all day watching television!

_____

b My car keeps breaking down.

_____

c I just can't get to sleep these days.

_____

d Since my father retired, he doesn't know what to do with himself.

_____

e I just don't know what to do with my hair. It looks awful!

_____

8 *mustn't* or *don't have to*?

Underline the correct verb form.

Example
We have a lot of work tomorrow.
You *mustn't*/*don't have to* be late.

a You *mustn't*/*don't have to* tell Mary what I told you. It's a secret.

b The museum is free. You *mustn't*/*don't have to* pay to get in.

c Children *mustn't*/*don't have to* tell lies. It's very naughty.

d Terry's a millionaire. He *mustn't*/*doesn't have to* go to work.

e I *mustn't*/*don't have to* do my washing. My mother does it for me.

f We *mustn't*/*don't have to* rush. We've got plenty of time.

g You *mustn't*/*don't have to* play with guns. They're dangerous.

h This is my favourite pen. You can borrow it, but you *mustn't*/*don't have to* lose it.

i 'Shall I come with you?'
'You can if you want, but you *mustn't*/*don't have to*.'

Vocabulary and pronunciation

9 Nationality words

1 T.25 Complete the chart with the country and the nationality adjective. Notice that all nationality words have capital letters in English!
*the french *the english
Put in the stress marks.

Country	Adjective
'Italy	I'talian
'Germany	
	Greek
'England	
'Finland	
	Dutch
	Chi'nese
	'Scottish (Scotch is a drink!)

2 T.26 Match the people with a suitable sentence about them. Notice the stress marks.

The I'talians — had many great philosophers.

The Greeks — grow lots of tulips.

The 'Germans — like taking saunas.

The Dutch — wear kilts.

The 'English — are good at business.

The Chi'nese — talk a lot about the weather.

The Finns — eat a lot of pasta.

The Scots — cook lots of noodles.

⚠️
1 If the adjective ends with the sounds /s/, /z/, /ʃ/, or /tʃ/, there is no -s at the end of the word that refers to the people.
English   The English
but
German   The Germans

2 Sometimes the word for the people is different from the adjective.
Finnish   The Finns
Scottish   The Scots

3 T.27 Complete the chart and mark the stress.
Add some countries of your own choice at the end.

Country	Adjective	A sentence about the people
Wales	*Welsh*	*The Welsh love rugby.*
'Ireland		
Spain		
Ja'pan		
'Russia		
'Sweden		
'Switzerland		
'Mexico		
Au'stralia		
'Turkey		

Pronunciation

10 Correcting wrong information

1 **T.28** Read the telephone conversation between Mrs Maddox and Mr Hardcastle, her bank manager. In each line of the conversation, Mr Hardcastle gives some wrong information and Mrs Maddox corrects him.

Mark the main stressed word or words in Mrs Maddox's replies like this •.

Mr H Good morning Miss Maddox.

Mrs M It's Mrs Maddox actually.

Mr H Oh yes. Mrs Mary Maddox of …

Mrs M Mrs Maureen Maddox.

Mr H Yes, of course. Maureen Maddox of twenty-three …

Mrs M Twenty-two, actually.

Mr H Twenty-two Hillside Lane, Chesterfield.

Mrs M Hillside Road, Chesterfield.

Mr H Ah yes. Now Mrs Maddox, I believe you want to borrow five hundred pounds.

Mrs M No, in fact, I want to borrow five thousand pounds. Haven't you got my letter?

Mr H No, I'm afraid not. But I understand you want to open a music shop for your son.

Mrs M Oh, dear me, no. I want to open a gift shop for my daughter. Don't you think you should read my letter, Mr Hardcastle?

Mr H A gift shop for your daughter. Well, I'll send you a form to …

Mrs M But you sent me a form last week, and I'm ringing because I have some queries about it.

Mr H Oh, so you've filled in the form …

Mrs M No, I haven't filled in the form. I can't fill it in because I don't understand it. That's why I'm ringing.

Mr H Oh I see! You want to ask me some questions about the form.

Mrs M Not any more. I don't want to ask you questions about anything!! Good bye!

2 Practise reading the conversation aloud.

Multi-word verbs

11 Separable or inseparable?

1 Notice how a dictionary shows you if a multi-word verb can be separated by an object or not.

> **turn sth on** to move the switch, etc on a piece of machinery, etc to start it working: *Turn the lights on!*

The particle (*on*) comes after **sth**. This means the verb and the particle can be separated.

***Turn** the light **on**.*   ***Turn on** the light.*

If the object is a pronoun (*it, him, her, me, them, us, you*), it must come before the particle.

*Turn **it** on.*   NOT *~~Turn on it.~~*

> **call for sb/sth** (*Brit*) to collect: *I'll call for you when it's time to go.*

The particle (*for*) comes before **sb/sth**. This means the verb and the particle cannot be separated.

*I'll **call for** John later.*   *I'll **call for** him.*

But NOT *~~I'll call him for.~~*

2 **T.29** Use your dictionary to see if the multi-word verbs in the exercise are separable or not. Put the word *it* into the correct place in the sentences.

> Example
> You must be very hot with your coat on.
> Why don't you take __it__ off ___ ?

a The music is too loud! Turn ___ down ___ !

b You can borrow my camera, but you must look ___ after ___ .

c I haven't read the newspaper yet. Don't throw ___ away ___ .

d My shirt is filthy! Look ___ at ___ !

e It'll be a great party! I'm really looking forward ___ to ___ .

f Is that story true, or did you make ___ up ___ ?

g I saw a lovely jumper today. I tried ___ on ___ but it was too small.

h Don't drop your litter in the street! Pick ___ up ___ !

i You can't have my dictionary. Give ___ back ___ to me!

j 'What's the answer to this question?'

'Don't ask me. Work ___ out ___ for yourself!'

5 Future forms
somebody, nobody, anybody, everybody

1 *will* or *going to*?

T.30 Complete the dialogues using a form of *will* or *going to*, and any other necessary words. Sometimes both future forms are possible.

Example
'Why are you wearing your old clothes?'
'Because I'm _*going to wash*_ the car.'

a 'I've got a headache. Have you got any aspirin?'

'Yes. It's in the bathroom. I _____ it for you.'

b 'Don't forget to tell me if I can help you.'

'Thank you. I _____ a ring if I think of anything.'

c 'Why are you making sandwiches?'

'Because we _____ a picnic on the beach.'

'What a lovely idea! I _____ the towels and the swimming costumes.'

d 'I'm going now! Bye!'
'Bye! What time _____ you _____ back tonight?'

'I don't know. I _____ phone you later.'

e 'Who do you think _____ win the next election?'
'The Labour Party _____ win, definitely.'

f 'You still owe me ten pounds. Have you forgotten?'

'I'm sorry. Yes, I'd forgotten. I _____ back tomorrow.'

g 'Wow, Pete! What a lovely new bike!'
'It's good, isn't it?'
'Pete … I was wondering. What _____ do with your old bike?'
'I don't know. Why? Do you want it?'
'Er … well, maybe.'
'Fine. You can have it.'

'I _____ you for it. How much do you want?'
'It's OK. You can have it for nothing.'

h 'Your exams start in two weeks' time.
When _____ you _____ start revising? You haven't done any yet.'
'I know. I'll do some tonight.'
'You're going out tonight.'

'I _____ tomorrow night, then.'

i 'Can you repair my watch, please?'
'Certainly.'
'How much _____ it _____ cost?'
'I charge twenty pounds an hour.'

'That's fine. When _____ it _____ ready?'
'Friday morning.'
'Lovely.'

j 'Do you like the shirt I bought for Peter's birthday?'
'Mmm. I'm sure he _____ . What _____ you _____ do for his birthday?'
'We're going out for a meal.'

2 Where are they going?

Look at the pictures. Where are the people going? Write questions and answers, using *going* + verb + *-ing*.

a _____

Example
Where's he going?
He's going swimming.

b _____

c _____

d _____

e _____

3 I'm sure they'll …

Complete the sentences using *will* or *won't* and any other necessary words.

Example
Mary's been working very hard for her exams.
I'm sure ___she'll pass the exams easily___ .

a If you don't feel well, go to bed and rest. I'm sure

you _____ soon.

b Ask John if you have problems with your

homework. I'm sure _____ you.

c I'll ask my sister for some money, but I know she

_____ . She's really mean.

d You don't need your umbrella today. I don't think

_____ .

e I can't read small writing any more. I think I

_____ soon.

f Don't sit in the sun for too long.

You _____ .

g Don't try that new restaurant. I'm sure

you _____ .

h It's my driving test soon, but I know I

_____ . I haven't had enough

lessons.

4 Making offers

T.31 Make offers with *I'll* for the following situations.

Example
'It's so hot in this room!'
I'll open the window.

a I'm dying for a drink!

_____

b There's someone at the door.

_____

c I haven't got any money.

_____

d I need to be at the station in ten minutes.

_____ a lift.

e My suitcases are so heavy!

_____

5 Making arrangements

1 **T.32** Complete the conversation with verbs in the Present Continuous. Use each of the verbs in the box *once* only. Read the dialogue to the end before you start.

invite	stay	come	have	make
get	book	give	travel	deliver

Ssh! Can you keep a secret?

A Can you keep a secret?

B Yes, of course. What is it?

A I (**a**) _____ a surprise party for Rosa. Next Saturday. It's her thirtieth birthday.

B A surprise party! That'll be difficult to arrange without her knowing. Who (**b**) _____ you _____?

A Everybody. All our friends, her friends from work, all her family, even her two aunts from Scotland. They (**c**) _____ down by train on Friday evening and they (**d**) _____ overnight in that small hotel at the end of our road.

B What about the food and drink? Where (**e**)_____ you _____ that from?

A It's all arranged. Marcello's restaurant (**f**) _____ all kinds of food and drink on Saturday afternoon, and their chef (**g**) _____ even _____ a special birthday cake with pink icing and sugar flowers.

B Excellent! And what (**h**) _____ you _____ Rosa for her birthday? Have you got her a good present?

A Oh yes! I (**i**) _____ a very special holiday. A weekend for two in Paris! We (**j**) _____ by Euro Star, through the Euro Tunnel!

B That's a great idea. Very clever! I can see that you are going to enjoy her birthday, too! Am I invited to this party?

A Of course. But keep it a secret!

2 All the future forms in the dialogue could be expressed by the *going to* future as well, but one example does not sound very natural. Which is it?

6 Choosing the correct form

In the following pairs of responses, one verb form is right and one is wrong. Put a tick (✔) for the correct response and a (✗) for the wrong one.

a 'Have you booked your holiday?'
- ☐ 'Yes, we have. We're going to Italy.'
- ☐ 'Yes, we have. We'll go to Italy.'

b

'Have you got toothache again?'

- ☐ 'Oooh! It's agony! But I see the dentist this afternoon.'
- ☐ 'Oooh! It's agony! But I'm seeing the dentist this afternoon.'

c 'What a beautiful day! Not a cloud in the sky!'
- ☐ 'Ah, but the weather forecast says it's raining.'
- ☐ 'Ah, but the weather forecast says it's going to rain.'

d 'I thought you had just bought a fax machine.'
- ☐ 'Yes, that's right. It's being delivered tomorrow.'
- ☐ 'Yes, that's right. It will be delivered tomorrow.'

e 'Please don't tell anyone. It's a secret.'
- ☐ 'Don't worry. We won't tell anybody.'
- ☐ 'Don't worry. We're not telling anybody.'

f

'I haven't got enough money to pay for my ticket.'

- ☐ 'It's OK. I'm going to lend you some.'
- ☐ 'It's OK. I'll lend you some.'

g 'You two look really shocked. What's the matter?'
- ☐ 'We've just learnt that we'll have twins!'
- ☐ 'We've just learnt that we're going to have twins!'

h 'Can you meet me after work?'
- ☐ 'I'd love to, but John's taking me out tonight.'
- ☐ 'I'd love to, but John'll take me out tonight.'

somebody, nobody, anybody, everybody

7 Compound words

> ⚠

1   Look at the sentences from the text about the Schumacher's holiday on page 52 of the Student's book.

> If **something** is a hundred years old, that's pretty old.
>
> **Everyone** we've met has been real nice.
>
> Did I forget **anything**?

2   Look at the compounds that can be formed.

some		one
any	+	body
no		thing
every		where

3   In general, we use *some* in positive sentences and *any* in negatives and questions, but not always.
   – In offers and requests we usually use *some*.

> Would you like **something** to eat?
> Can I have **something** to drink?

   – We use *some* when we expect the answer 'yes'.

> Is there **somebody** I can speak to?
> Can we go **somewhere** quiet?

4   We generally use *any* after *if*.

> If you need **anything**, just ask.

5   *Any* has another meaning. It can mean *it doesn't matter who/where/what …*

> Come and see me **anytime** you want. I don't mind.
> Help yourself to food. You can have **anything** you want.
> **Anyone** will tell you that two and two is four.

Put one of the compounds into each gap.

a   Does _____ want a game of tennis?

b   What's that smell? Can you smell _____ burning?

c   I asked if _____ wanted an ice-cream, but _____ did, so I just bought one for myself.

d   Did _____ phone me while I was out?

e   Your face looks terribly familiar. Haven't I seen you _____ before?

f   She left the room without saying _____ .

g   This doesn't look a very nice restaurant. Can we go _____ else?

h   I have _____ more to say to you. Goodbye.

i   I have never been _____ more beautiful than Scotland.

j   I felt so embarrassed. I was sure that _____ was looking at me.

k   'What do you want for supper?'

   '_____ . I don't mind.'

l   It was Sunday, and the town was deserted.

   _____ was in the streets, and _____ was open.

m   'Who was at the party?'

   '_____ . Pete, Anna, James, Kathy, all the Smiths, Sally Beams and Sally Rogers.'

n   'Where do you want to go on holiday?'

   '_____ hot. I don't care if it's Greece, Spain, Italy or the Sahara, but it's got to be hot.'

8 *make* or *do*?

1 Which words and expressions go with *make*? Which go with *do*? Write them in the correct column.

make		do
a mistake		*my homework*

a mistake
my homework
the shopping
up my mind
a mess
a complaint
someone a favour
sure that
the housework
my bed
nothing
my best
money
a speech
business with
a profit
exercises
a noise
a phone call
friends with
a will
the washing-up
love
progress

2 Complete the sentences using one of the expressions in Exercise 1 in the correct form.

a Is there a public call box near here? I have to

_____ .

b First she said 'Yes', then she said 'No', but in the

end she _____ to marry him.

c When you're not sure what to do the best thing is to

_____ .

d Ssh! You mustn't _____ . The baby's asleep.

e My teacher says I must work harder, but I can't

work any harder, I'm _____ .

f We asked to see the manager and we _____

_____ about the terrible service in the restaurant.

g At first I found learning English very easy, but now

I don't think I'm _____ any _____ at all!

h Could you _____ please? Could you give me a lift to the airport?

i My uncle died without _____ and it was very difficult for our family to sort out his money and possessions.

j We have some lovely new neighbours; we've already

_____ with them.

k I like to keep fit, so I _____ every day.

l Before you go on holiday you should _____

_____ that all the doors and windows are shut and locked.

m _____ , not war!

Prepositions

9 *in*, *at*, *on* for place

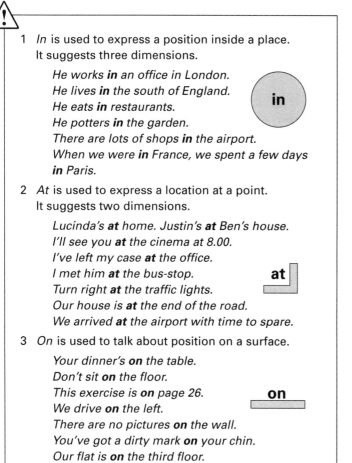

1 *In* is used to express a position inside a place.
It suggests three dimensions.

> He works **in** an office **in** London.
> He lives **in** the south of England.
> He eats **in** restaurants.
> He potters **in** the garden.
> There are lots of shops **in** the airport.
> When we were **in** France, we spent a few days **in** Paris.

2 *At* is used to express a location at a point.
It suggests two dimensions.

> Lucinda's **at** home. Justin's **at** Ben's house.
> I'll see you **at** the cinema at 8.00.
> I've left my case **at** the office.
> I met him **at** the bus-stop.
> Turn right **at** the traffic lights.
> Our house is **at** the end of the road.
> We arrived **at** the airport with time to spare.

3 *On* is used to talk about position on a surface.

> Your dinner's **on** the table.
> Don't sit **on** the floor.
> This exercise is **on** page 26.
> We drive **on** the left.
> There are no pictures **on** the wall.
> You've got a dirty mark **on** your chin.
> Our flat is **on** the third floor.

Put *in*, *at*, or *on* into each gap.

a I met my husband _____ Italy. He was _____ a shop, buying pasta. I was _____ a queue, waiting to buy some bread.

b Last night I was _____ the kitchen when I lost my glasses. I looked _____ all the shelves and _____ all the cupboards. I thought I'd put them _____ one of the drawers, but they weren't there. They certainly weren't _____ the table or _____ the floor. Had I left them _____ work? Were they _____ the car? Then I realized where they were. They were _____ my nose.

c 'Where were you at 2.00?'

'_____ the beach.' '_____ work.' '_____ Manchester.'

'_____ Sally's house doing my homework.'

'_____ the bath.' '_____ home.' '_____ a boat.'

Pronunciation

10 Vowel sounds and spelling

1 **T.33** Put a circle around the symbol that matches the sound in the underlined letters. They are all single vowel sounds.

Example
w<u>o</u>rd /ʌ/ ⟨ɜ:⟩ /ɔ:/

a w<u>ea</u>ther /e/ /iː/ /æ/
b s<u>u</u>gar /uː/ /ʊ/ /ʌ/
c w<u>o</u>man /ɒ/ /ɪ/ /ʊ/
d w<u>o</u>men /ɒ/ /ɪ/ /ʊ/
e <u>u</u>ncle /ʌ/ /æ/ /ɒ/
f h<u>al</u>f /ɑː/ /æ/ /ɔ:/

2 **T.34** Cross out the word which does not contain the vowel sound on the left.

Example
/ɪ/ build ~~field~~ fill women

a /e/ leather friend break bread
b /ʌ/ front rough won't country
c /ɒ/ clock wonder want wash
d /æ/ angry hungry fax salmon
e /iː/ cheese breath meal breathe
f /uː/ spoon wooden zoo souvenir
g /ɔ:/ warm walk store work
h /ɜ:/ world ferry early journalist

3 **T.35** Transcribe the following words.

Example
/ˈkʌbəd/ *cupboard*

a /ˈpetrəl/ _____
b /ˈjɒgət/ _____
c /ˈɪntrəstɪŋ/_____
d /θɔ:t/ _____
e /ˈbrekfəst/ _____
f /ˈstætʃu:/ _____
g /ˈfri:zɪŋ/ _____
h /ˈlʌkʃərɪ/ _____
i /ˈdɔ:tə/ _____
j /ˈsmu:ð/ _____

6

like as a verb
like as a preposition
Relative clauses

like

1 Questions with *like*

1 Answer the questions about yourself.

a What do you like doing most in your English class?

   _____.

b Do you like working alone or with a partner?

   _____.

c Would you like to have more or less homework
   after class?

   _____.

d What's your classroom like?

   _____.

e What are your classmates like?

   _____.

f What is your spoken English like?

   _____.

g Would you like to speak more or write more in class?

   _____.

2 Write suitable questions for the following answers,
using *What … like?, Do … like …?,
Would … like …?, or How …?, What/Who … look like?*

Examples
What's the weather like?
It's raining again!

Do you like cooking?
No, I don't. I can't even boil an egg!

a _____?

   It's boring and the hours are so long. 8.30 in the
   morning until 6.00 at night. I'm looking for another
   one.

b _____?

   In my family? Well, everybody says I look like my
   mother but I think I look more like my father.

c _____?

   Oh, I looked awful! Really ugly! I was fat and spotty
   until I was 16!

d _____?

   Coffee, please. I don't like tea.

e _____?

   Yes, I love it. I play every weekend in summer.

f _____?

   Yes, I'd love to. What time does the film start?

g _____?

   We've only had one lesson with her, but she seems
   very nice. Much less strict than Mr Winter was.

h _____?

   My father's away in Poland at the moment. But
   they're both very well, thank you. I'll tell them you
   asked about them.

3 **T.36** Read through the conversation between two old friends. Then fill the gaps with a suitable question.

A I'm applying for a job in East Africa.
B Are you? I used to live there. In Tanzania. I was there about ten years ago.
A Really !
 (**a**) What _____ ?
B It was really interesting. I was there for two years. I liked everything except the climate.
A Why? (**b**) _____ that _____ ?
B Well, I was on the coast, in Dar es Salaam, so it was very hot and humid all of the time.
A And the people, (**c**) _____ ?
B Very nice. Very kind. And of the course the Masai people look wonderful.
A (**d**) _____ ?
B Well, they're very tall and they wear the most amazing coloured beads, in their hair, round their necks, on their arms and legs. And the unmarried men put red mud in their hair. They're a magnificent sight.
A I suppose you went on safari when you were there.
 (**e**) _____ that _____ ?
B It was very exciting. I went to the Serengeti Plain and the Ngoro Ngoro Crater.
A (**f**) Which animals _____ best?
B Actually, I think it was the giraffes. They were so graceful, so elegant – but I liked all the animals. (**g**) What _____ _____ to see if you go there?
A The lions, of course. Especially those that live in the trees. I hope I get the job. It's been great talking to you.
B And you. Give me a ring and let me know what happens.

2 *like* versus *would like*

1 Match a line in **A** with a line in **B**.

A	B
a I only like white chocolate.	I'd love one. I'm very thirsty.
b Would you like a lift?	I hate him.
c Would you like some more cake?	I'd love to. That's very kind.
d Would you like a cold drink?	I'd love some. It's delicious.
e Don't you like your boss?	I don't. I can't stand it.
f I don't like cabbage.	Nor would I.
g I wouldn't like to work for her!	Nothing.
h Would you like to come to dinner?	Really? I love it.
i What do you like doing at the weekends?	It's OK. I'll get the bus.

2 **T.37** In **A**'s questions in the following dialogues, one question is right and one is wrong. Put a tick (✔) next to the right one and a cross (✗) next to the wrong one.

a **A** ☐ What do you like to do tonight?
  ☐ What would you like to do tonight?
 B Something a bit different. I feel like a change.

b **A** ☐ Where do you like going on holiday?
  ☐ Where would you like to go on holiday?
 B We usually go skiing in winter, then somewhere hot in summer.

c **A** ☐ Do you like Coke?
  ☐ Would you like a Coke?
 B Yes, please.

d **A** ☐ What sort of books do you like reading?
  ☐ What sort of books would you like to read?
 B Science fiction and detective stories. But I don't read much.

e **A** ☐ Do you like your teacher?
  ☐ Would you like to be a teacher?
 B She's OK.

f **A** ☐ Do you like your teacher?
  ☐ Would you like to be a teacher?
 B I couldn't stand it!

3 *like* versus *as*

> 1 When *like* is used as a preposition, it is always followed by a noun. It means *similar to/the same as/for example.*
>
>   *I look **like** my mother.*
>
>   *They have so many animals. Their house is **like** a zoo.*
>
>   *'What star sign are you?' 'I'm Gemini, **like** you.'*
>
>   *'You're stupid.' 'Why do you say things **like** that?'*
>
>   *Their children are loud and bossy. I don't like kids **like** that.*
>
> 2 *As* can also be used as a preposition followed by a noun. It expresses the job, function or use of a person or a thing.
>
>   *I worked **as** a waitress over the holidays.*
>   *We use our garage **as** a storage place.*
>   *She went to a party dressed **as** a nun.*
>
> 3 When *as* is used as a conjunction, it is followed by a subject and a verb.
>
>   *Do **as** I say and sit down.*
>
>   *Don't eat and speak at the same time, **as** my mother used to say.*
>
>   ***As** you know, we're leaving tomorrow at 10.00.*
>
>   Notice the use of *as* in *as usual.*
>
>   *Pat and Peter arrived late, **as** usual.*
>
> 4 We also use *as* in comparisons.
>
>   *My daughter is **as** tall **as** me.*
>   *She works in the same office **as** me.*

Put *as* or *like* into each gap.

a I'll be back in touch ____ soon ____ possible.

b This wine tastes ____ vinegar!

c I've known Andy for years. He went to the same school ____ I did.

d My sister's a teacher, ____ me.

e 'We had a new teacher today called Mary.'
'What was she ____ ?'

f Who do I look ____ , my mother or my father?

g She really annoys me. I can't stand people ____ her.

h I'll see you tomorrow at 11.00, ____ usual.

i It's July and the weather's awful! It's ____ winter!

j I need to buy all sorts of things ____ socks, shirts and knickers.

k My wife has found a job ____ a personal assistant.

l Dave drinks ____ a fish! I've never seen anyone drink as much.

m My brother has a car ____ yours.

n Don't touch anything. Leave everything ____ it is.

o It's freezing. My feet are ____ blocks of ice.

Verb patterns

4 Choosing the correct form

T.38 Put a tick (✔) next to the correct form of the verb.

a I want
☐ you be
☐ you to be
☐ that you are
more careful with your homework in future.

b I stopped
☐ to smoke
☐ smoke
☐ smoking
when I was thirty.

c Why did I agree
☐ to work
☐ work
☐ working
with you? I can't stand it.

d I tried
☐ tell you
☐ to tell you
☐ telling
that you were making a mistake, but you wouldn't listen.

e I'm looking forward
☐ to see
☐ to seeing
☐ seeing
you again soon.

f My parents let me
☐ do
☐ to do
☐ doing
what I wanted when I was young.

g I wasn't allowed
☐ going
☐ go
☐ to go
out unless they knew where I was going.

h I finished
☐ watching
☐ to watch
☐ watch
the television, and then I went to bed.

5 A puzzle

Complete the sentences with a verb from the box.
You need either the *-ing* form or the infinitive.
Write your answers in the puzzle.
The vertical words spell what we all like to eat (9, 4)!

count	invite	touch	pull	wish	complain
speak	wash	feed	defrost	stand	find	fill

a   I hate _____ in a queue. It's such a waste of time.

b   My baby daughter is just learning to _____ .
    She can say two words – 'Mama' and 'pussy'.

c   Can you remember to _____ up the car with
    petrol? It's nearly empty.

d   I'd love to _____ Dave and Maggie round for
    a meal some time.

e   I couldn't sleep last night. I tried _____
    sheep, but that didn't help.

f   My jeans need _____ . They're filthy.

g   The customer tried to _____ about the service
    in the restaurant, but the waiter refused to listen to him.

h   Stop _____ my hair! It hurts!

i   I just want to _____ you Happy Birthday.

j   Would you mind _____ our cat while we're
    away on holiday?

k   When you go round a museum, you aren't allowed to
    _____ anything.

l   Don't forget to_____ the chicken before you
    cook it.

m   Did you manage to _____ what you were looking for?

6 Using a dictionary

Look at the extracts from the *Oxford Wordpower
Dictionary*. They show you which verb patterns
are possible. Some of the verb patterns in the
sentences are right, and some are wrong. Tick (✔)
those that are right, and correct the wrong ones.

> ☆ **like** ¹ /laɪk/ *verb* [T] **1** to find sb/sth pleasant; to
> be fond of sb/sth: *He's nice. I like him a lot.* ○ *Do
> you like their new flat?* ○ *I like my coffee with
> milk.* ○ *I like playing tennis.* ○ *She didn't like it
> when I shouted at her.* ☛ The opposite is **dis-
> like**. When **like** means 'have the habit of...' or
> 'think it's a good thing to...', it is followed by
> the infinitive: *I like to get up early so that I can
> go for a run before breakfast.* Look at **likes and
> dislikes. 2** to want: *Do what you like. I don't
> care.* ☛ **Would like** is a more polite way to say
> 'want': *Would you like to come to lunch on Sun-
> day?* ○ *I would like some more cake, please.* ○ *I'd
> like to speak to the manager.* **Would like** is
> always followed by the infinitive, never by the
> *-ing* form. **3** (in negative sentences) to be un-
> willing to do sth: *I didn't like to disturb you
> while you were eating.*

a   ☐   We like going out to eat in restaurants.

b   ☐   Would you like coming round to our
        house for a meal some time?

c   ☐   I like it when you tickle my feet.

d   ☐   I like to go to the dentist's twice a year.

e   ☐   I'd like to make a complaint.

f   ☐   I always like paying my bills on time.

> ☆ **agree** /ə'griː/ *verb* **1** [I,T] **agree (with sb/
> sth); agree (that...)** to have the same opinion
> as sb/sth: *'I think we should talk to the manager
> about this.' 'Yes, I agree.'* ○ *I agree with Paul.* ○
> *Do you agree that we should travel by train?* ○
> *I'm afraid I don't agree.* ☛ Look at **disagree.
> 2** [I] **agree (to sth)** to say yes to sth: *I asked if I
> could go home early and she agreed.* ○ *Andrew
> has agreed to lend me his car for the weekend.*
> ☛ Look at **refuse** ¹. **3** [I,T] **agree (to do sth);
> agree (on sth)** to make an arrangement or
> agreement with sb: *They agreed to meet again
> the following day.* ○ *Can we agree on a price?* ○
> *We agreed a price of £500.* **4** [I] **agree with sth**
> to think that sth is right: *I don't agree with ex-
> periments on animals.* **5** [I] to be the same as
> sth: *The two accounts of the accident do not
> agree.*

g   ☐   He thinks we should go, and I'm agree.

h   ☐   She thinks she's right, but I'm not agree.

i   ☐   I don't agree with you.

j   ☐   Most scientists agree that global warming
        is a serious problem.

k   ☐   She thought we should go, and I agreed it.

l   ☐   They agreed discussing the problem
        further.

Relative clauses

7 Subject or object?

Tick (✔) the sentences where the relative pronoun is necessary. If it is possible to leave out the relative pronoun, cross it out.

Examples
I don't like people who arrive late. ✔
The company ~~that~~ he works for is based in Germany.

a Where are the scissors that I bought yesterday?

b I want you to meet the woman who taught me how to drive.

c The meal that you cooked was delicious.

d I like animals that don't make a mess.

e The film that I've always wanted to see is on TV tonight.

f The flat that they bought was very expensive.

g The room in our house that is most used is the kitchen.

h I didn't like the meal that we had yesterday.

i The people who work here are very interesting.

j The man who you were talking about has just come in the room.

8 Gap filling

Fill the gaps with *who, which, where, whose,* or *that.*
Where possible, leave out the relative pronoun.

a I received a letter this morning _____ really upset me.

b Toby, a boy _____ I went to school with, is ill in hospital.

c He's going to have an operation _____ could save his life.

d Toby, _____ parents both died a few years ago, is the same age as me.

e I recently went back to the town _____ I was born.

f The people _____ used to live next door moved a long time ago.

g I met a girl _____ I used to go out with.

h She told me a story _____ I found hard to believe.

i She said she'd married a man _____ had been married ten times before.

j Apparently, he lost all his money gambling,

_____ really annoyed her.

Vocabulary

9 Antonyms and synonyms

1 Write the opposite.

Examples
an old house   *a new house*
an old man   *a young man*

a a single person   _____

  a single ticket   _____

b a strong man   _____

  strong beer   _____

c a rich person   _____

  rich food   _____

d a sweet apple   _____

  sweet wine   _____

e a hot curry   _____

  a hot drink   _____

f dark hair   _____

  a dark room   _____

2 Write another adjective with a similar meaning.

Examples
a pretty girl   *an attractive girl*
a handsome man   *a good-looking man*

a a rich woman   _____

b a funny story   _____

c a well-dressed person   _____

d an untidy room   _____

e a badly-behaved child   _____

f accurate information   _____

g friendly people   _____

h a silly person   _____

i a clever person   _____

j a wonderful idea   _____

k awful news   _____

l disgusting food   _____

Multi-word verbs

10 Multi-word verbs + objects

1 Some separable multi-word verbs have a strong association with a certain object.

> Examples
> *turn off a light/the television*
> *work out the answers*

Match a verb in **A** with an object in **B**.

A	B
sort out	clothes in a shop
put out	children
fill in	a meeting to another time
find out	a problem
try on	a mess
try out	clothes in a cupboard
bring up	a form
clear up	something you don't want to a shop
take back	a new idea, a new drug
put off	a fire
put away	information

2 **T.39** Complete the sentences with one of the multi-word verbs in its correct form.

a I'll dry the dishes if you _____ them_____ .
I don't know where they go.

b 'Can you _____ the time of the next train to London?'
'OK. I'll phone the station.'

c 'Look at these shoes! They're brand new, and the heel's fallen off already.'

' _____ them _____ and change them, then.'

d 'Oh, dear! The washing machine isn't working, I haven't got any clean clothes, and I've got to go to work. What am I going to do?'

'Don't worry. I'll _____ it all _____ . Just go to work.'

e The fire was so intense that it took the firemen three hours to _____ it _____ .

f The government wants to _____ a new scheme to encourage people to start their own businesses.

g 'Can I _____ these jeans _____ , please?'
'Sure. The changing rooms are over there.'

h I won't be able to go shopping with you today, I'm afraid. I've got a lot on at the moment.

Can we _____ it _____ till next week?

i I don't mind you baking a cake, but just make sure you _____ everything _____ when you've finished.

j 'What should I do with this form?'

' _____ it _____ .'

Pronunciation

11 Sentence stress

T.40 What did **A** say? Read **B**'s responses, noting the main stressed word, and write what **A** said.

> Example
> **A** *Anna's got long, blonde hair.*
>
> **B** No, she hasn't. Anna's got short, blonde hair.

a **A** _____ .

  B No, he isn't. Jack's very tall.

b **A** _____ ?

  B No, I don't. I want a return ticket.

c **A** _____ ?

  B No, she doesn't. Liz likes white wine.

d **A** _____ ?

  B No, he didn't say that. He said the film was interesting.

e **A** _____ ?

  B No, they don't. Jane and Paul hate going for walks.

f **A** _____ ?

  B No, I wouldn't. I'd like a cold drink, please.

g **A** _____ .

  B Well, I hated school when I was a child.

h **A** _____ ?

  B No, I haven't. I've got a stomach ache.

7 Present Perfect Tense review

Present Perfect

1 *How many did she ...? How many has she ...?*

1 Complete the questions about the people.

Sylvia Conran
1942–

a How many books
_____ ?

Jane Austen
1775–1817

b How many books
_____ ?

Sonja Samms
1973–

c How many films
_____ ?

Marilyn Monroe
1926–1962

d How many films
_____ ?

Bob Marley
1945–1981

e How many records
_____ ?

Andy Cushing
1966–

f How many records
_____ ?

David Hockney
1937–

g How many pictures
_____ ?

Van Gogh
1853–1890

h How many pictures
_____ ?

2 Who are the sentences referring to?
Write a letter **a–h** next to each one.

☐ She has recently married her co-star, Richard Ledmann.

☐ He has lived in Los Angeles for many years because he prefers the light there.

☐ She has just published a biography of Charles Dickens.

☐ He has played with three different bands over the years.

☐ She committed suicide in 1962.

☐ His band was called *The Wailers*.

☐ She never married.

☐ He only sold one painting while he was alive.

3 Ask questions about the first four sentences in Exercise 2.

a Where _____ get married?

b Why _____ to Los Angeles?

c How long _____ her to write it?

d How old _____ started to play the guitar?

4 What are the two different tenses used in Exercises 1–3?

2 Choosing the correct tense

David Hockney, *A Bigger Splash*

In the text about David Hockney, tick (✔) the box
for the correct tense.

a David Hockney ☐ born ☐ is born ☐ was born in 1937 in Bradford, a town in the north of England.

b He ☐ is ☐ was ☐ has been interested in painting and design all his life.

c He ☐ studies ☐ has studied ☐ studied at the Royal College of Art from 1959–62.

d Over the past twenty years, he ☐ has travelled ☐ travels ☐ travelled to most parts of the world.

e He first ☐ went ☐ has gone ☐ has been to America when he was twenty-five.

f His most famous work is called *A Bigger Splash,* which ☐ painted ☐ has painted ☐ was painted in 1967.

g Hockney ☐ also designed ☐ has also designed ☐ is also designed stage sets and books.

h He ☐ lives ☐ has lived ☐ lived in Los Angeles for many years.

i He ☐ never married. ☐ has never married. ☐ is never married.

j He ☐ lives ☐ has lived ☐ lived with friends in a villa in the mountains above Los Angeles.

3 Dialogues

T.41 Write the dialogues using the cues.

a **A** You/be/brown! Where/you/be?

_____

B We/be/on holiday.

_____

A Where/you/go?

_____

B We/go/Spain.

_____

A When/you/get back?

_____

B Last night. The plane/land/6.00 in the evening.

_____

b **A** What/you/do/to your finger?

_____

B I/cut/myself.

_____

A How/you/do that?

_____

B I/cook/and the knife/slip.

_____

A you/put/anything on it?

_____

B No. It's not that bad.

4 *been* or *gone*?

> ⚠ Note the difference between *been* and *gone*.
>
> *She's **been** to Paris.*
> (Sometime in her life but she isn't there now.)
>
> *She's **gone** to Paris.* (She's there now.)

Put *been* or *gone* into each gap.

a 'Where's Peter?' 'He's _____ on holiday.'

b Where have you _____ ? You're so brown!

c 'Are you going to the shops this afternoon?'

   'No, I've already _____ . I went this morning.'

d 'Can I speak to Jenny, please?'

   'I'm afraid she's _____ to lunch. Can I take a message?'

e I've never _____ to Australia, but I'd like to go.

f 'When's your holiday?'

   'We've already _____ . We went to France.'

g 'Where's Harry these days?'

   'Didn't you know? He's _____ to another company.'

5 Time expressions

1 Put a tick (✔) if the time expression and the tense go together. Put a cross (✘) if they don't.

	Past Simple	Present Perfect
for	✔	✔
since	✘	✔
in (1960)		
ago		
at (8.00)		
just		
before		
yet		
already		
never		

2 Put the word in brackets in the most natural place in the sentence.

a I've heard you're getting married. (just)

b Have you read the newspaper? (yet)

c I've done my homework. (already)

d Have you been to Thailand? (ever)

e I haven't seen the film. (yet)

3 T.42 Write sentences for the situations, using *just*, *already*, or *yet*.

a You're having a drink. You put it down for a minute and the waiter takes your glass away.

   You say: Excuse me! _____ (not finish)

b You put out your cigarette two minutes ago. A friend offers you another cigarette.

   You say: No, thanks. _____ (put one out)

c John went out two minutes ago. The phone rings. It's someone for John.

   You say: _____ (go out)

d You fed the cat. Then your sister starts to feed the cat again.

   You say: _____ (feed her)

e You rush home because there's a football match on TV. You want to know if it's over.

   You ask: _____ (finish?)

6 Talking about you

Answer the questions about you.

a Have you been shopping recently?

b What did you buy?

c How much have you spent today?

d Have you had a busy day?

e Have you seen any good films recently?

f What lessons have you had today?

7 Correcting mistakes

Correct the mistakes in the sentences.

a How long do you know the teacher?

b This is the first time I eat honey with spaghetti.

c What have you done last night?

d I study English for four years.

e When have you got your hair cut?

f I have seen Peter yesterday.

8 Curriculum vitae

1 Read Henry's curriculum vitae.

CURRICULUM VITAE

Name	**Henry George Whitfield**
Address	22 Collier Lane
	Horsham
	Leeds LS3 6PT
Telephone	01532 27963
Date of birth	18 February 1974

Education

1983–92	Southfield High School, Leeds
1993–6	Nottingham University
	BA (Hons) English and Sociology
Languages	Fluent French
Computing skills	Microsoft Word

Work experience

April 1996 to present time	Working with disabled children in Botton Village, a community care centre near York.
1994–5	Secretary of the university climbing club, led a team to the Pyrenees.
July 1992– May 1993	Lived in Paris. Worked as a porter in a children's hospital. Acquired excellent French language skills.
October 1990– June1992	Worked at weekends as an assistant in a chemist's shop.
Interests	Travel, cinema, working with children, climbing.

---

2 **T.43** Complete the questions and answers in the conversation.

I Where _____ ?

H In Horsham near Leeds.

I _____ you _____ to university?

H Yes, I have. I _____to Nottingham University from 1993 to 1996.

I What subjects_____ ?

H _____ and _____ .

I _____ any languages?

H Yes, I do. I _____ fluently.

I _____ you ever _____ in France?

H Yes, I _____ . I _____ and _____ in Paris for a year.

I What kind of work _____ you _____ there?

H I _____ .

I What _____ now?

H I _____
near York.

I How long _____ there?

H Since _____ .

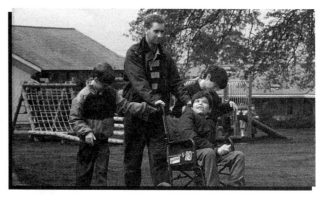

3 Complete the sentences about him below with suitable verbs in the correct tense.

a Henry _____ in 1974.

b He _____ in the village of Horsham near Leeds.

c He _____ English and Sociology at university.

d He _____ French when he _____ in Paris.

e He _____ with disabled children since April 1996.

f He _____ climbing and going to the cinema in his free time.

g When he was at school he _____ to work in a chemist's at weekends.

Present Perfect passive

9 Active or passive?

Underline the correct verb form in each of the following sentences.

a Tom *'s just promoted/'s just been promoted* to area manager of Eastern Europe.

b I *'ve applied/'ve been applied* for a new job.

c How many times *have you made/have you been made* redundant?

d Bob's wife *has just lost/has just been lost* her job.

e My father *has taken/has been taken* early retirement.

f My brother *has given/has been given* the sack. His boss said he was lazy.

g The number of people out of work *has risen/has been risen* to nearly 3 million.

h A strike *has called/has been called* by the air traffic controllers.

i They *haven't offered/haven't been offered* more money by the management.

j How much money *have you saved/have you been saved* for your retirement?

10 Two newspaper stories

1 Read the news stories and put the verbs in brackets into the correct tense, Present Perfect or Past Simple, active or passive.

THE LOCH NESS WALLET

14 years ago Spanish tourist Gaspar Sanchez **(a)** _____ (drop) his wallet into the waters of Loch Ness in Scotland. His passport, his car keys, his business card and his money **(b)** _____ (lose) in 150m of water. This week the phone **(c)** _____ (ring) in Señor Sanchez's Barcelona flat and a Scottish policeman told him, 'Sir, your wallet **(d)** _____ (find)!

It **(e)** _____ (discover) last Sunday on the bed of the loch by some scientists in a submarine looking for the Loch Ness monster!'

Señor Sanchez said, 'The whole thing is absolutely amazing. Apparently my wallet and its contents **(f)** _____ (put) in the post to me already. I should get them tomorrow. I can't believe it!'

Picassos taken in £40m raid

Swedish police **(a)** _____ just _____ (announce) that five paintings by Picasso **(b)** _____ (steal) from Stockholm's Modern Museum.

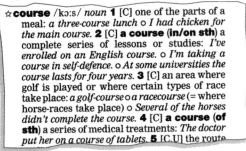

The paintings **(c)** _____ (value) by experts at 500 million kronor (about £40 million).

Police believe that they **(d)** _____ (take) early on Saturday evening, but for some reason the museum's burglar alarm **(e)** _____ (not go off) and the theft **(f)** _____ (not discover) until Monday morning. No clues **(g)** _____ so far _____ (find) at the scene of the crime.

2 Write the questions for the following answers.

a _____?
14 years ago.

b _____?
Last Sunday.

c _____?
Five paintings by Picasso.

d _____?
Yes, they have. At 500 million kronor, that's about £40 million.

e _____?
Saturday evening.

f _____?
No, none. Not yet.

Vocabulary

11 Words with more than one meaning

1 Many words have more than one meaning. Look at the dictionary entry for *course*. How many meanings do you know?

> ☆ **course** /kɔːs/ *noun* **1** [C] one of the parts of a meal: *a three-course lunch* ○ *I had chicken for the main course.* **2** [C] **a course (in/on sth)** a complete series of lessons or studies: *I've enrolled on an English course.* ○ *I'm taking a course in self-defence.* ○ *At some universities the course lasts for four years.* **3** [C] an area where golf is played or where certain types of race take place: *a golf-course* ○ *a racecourse* (= where horse-races take place) ○ *Several of the horses didn't complete the course.* **4** [C] **a course (of sth)** a series of medical treatments: *The doctor put her on a course of tablets.* **5** [C,U] the route

2 In the following sentences, the words in *italics* have more than one meaning. Find the correct definition in your dictionary. Find one other meaning.

a You've got a dirty *mark* on your shirt. Did you spill your food?

b How many political *parties* are there in your country?

c Where's the glue? I need to *stick* the handle back on this cup.

d Everyone has the *right* to live in peace.

e I'll check the departure board to see which platform the *train* leaves from.

f You gave her ten pounds, but you only gave me five. That's not *fair*!

g Some people are so *mean*. They just enjoy keeping their hands in their pockets.

h I'll put the picture up for you if you've got a hammer and a *nail*.

i We sat in the front *row* at the cinema, so we could see really well.

j It's common to *tip* waiters and taxi drivers 10%.

k My brother works for a *firm* of accountants.

Pronunciation

12 Phonetic script and word stress

1 T.44 Most of the following words in phonetic script are in Unit 7. Say them aloud to yourself, then transcribe them.

Example
/ˈmænɪdʒə/ *manager*

Two syllables	
a /ˈbɪznəs/	_____
b /fəˈget/	_____
c /əˈplaɪ/	_____
d /ˈfɒrən/	_____
e /ˈkɪdnæpt/	_____
f /kəˈrɪə/	_____
g /rɪˈzaɪn/	_____
h /rɪˈtaɪəd/	_____
i /ˈfæktri/	_____
j /dɪˈgriː/	_____

Three syllables	
k /ɪmˈplɔɪə/	_____
l /ɪmplɔɪˈiː/	_____
m /ˈɪntəvjuː/	_____
n /mɪljəˈneə/	_____
o /ˈpɒlətɪks/	_____
p /dɪˈrektə/	_____
q /ˈjuːnɪfɔːm/	_____
r /ˈmɜːdərə/	_____
s /rɪˈdʌndənt/	_____
t /ˌmægəˈziːn/	_____

Four syllables	
u /ˌʌnɪmˈplɔɪmənt/	_____
v /ˌɪntəvjuːˈiː/	_____
w /ˌpɒləˈtɪʃn/	_____
x /ˌæplɪˈkeɪʃn/	_____
y /ˌrezɪgˈneɪʃn/	_____
z /ɪnˈtɜːprɪtə/	_____

2 Which stress pattern does each word have?

●● ●	*a*
●● ●	*b*
●● ● ●	*k*
● ●●	
●● ●	
●● ● ●	
●● ● ●	
● ● ●●	

Prepositions

13 Noun + preposition

There are many nouns and prepositions that go together.
Fill the gaps with a preposition from the box.
Some are used more than once.

with for between on to out of in of about

a The factory workers are _____ strike because they want more money.

b Thousands of people are _____ work in this town. It's really difficult to get a job.

c I got a cheque _____ a hundred pounds this morning.

d You're really annoying me. You're doing it _____ purpose, aren't you?

e Can you tell the difference _____ butter and margarine?

f There have been a lot of complaints _____ your behaviour.

g The trouble _____ you is that you don't listen to anybody.

h I'm fed up with cooking. Let's eat out _____ a change.

i How much do you spend a week _____ average?

j Watch your step with Dad. He's _____ a terrible mood.

k Could you take a photo _____ me, please?

l I had a crash this morning. Fortunately I didn't do much damage _____ my car.

8

Conditionals
I'd rather …
wish and *If only*

---

1 Matching

Match a line in **A** with a line in **B** and a line in **C**.

A	B	C
a If we can afford it,	I'll be late for school.	You can put my supper in the oven.
b If you go to Paris,	step inside.	The views are fantastic.
c If I don't hear from you tomorrow,	tell him I never want to see him again.	The one we have now is very unreliable.
d If the pain gets too bad,	we'll buy a new car soon.	That should help.
e If the bus doesn't come soon,	I'll let you know.	That'll be the second time this week.
f If you can't see what you want in the window,	take another dose of painkillers.	And don't tell him where I've gone!
g If I'm going to be late,	you must go up the Eiffel Tower.	I need to speak to you again soon.
h If Peter rings,	I'll expect a call the next day.	There are lots more things to see in the shop.

2 Dialogues

T.45   Here are two dialogues mixed up. In one, Tom and Fran are talking about going shopping; in the other they are planning the menu for a barbecue. Sort them out and put them in the right order.

Shopping

- [a] Tom
- [ ] Fran
- [ ] Tom
- [ ] Fran
- [ ] Tom
- [ ] Fran
- [ ] Tom
- [ ] Fran
- [ ] Tom

Menu

- [b] Tom
- [ ] Fran
- [ ] Tom
- [ ] Fran
- [ ] Tom
- [ ] Fran
- [ ] Tom

a I'm going to the shops. Do you want anything?
b What shall we cook for supper when your sister comes? What does she eat?
c They're to go with my suit, so they need to be dark brown.
d That's a good idea. Let's do that.
e Erm … I'll try to find a pair of dark brown tights in the supermarket, but I'm not very good with colours.
f Sure. I'll do a raspberry pavlova.
g No, I don't think so. Oh, hang on. I need some tights.
h She likes most things, I think. Meat, fish …
i No, I won't.
j And another thing. If you're passing the post office, will you get some stamps?
k If I do the main course, will you do a dessert?
l OK. If I see some, I'll get them for you. What colour do you want?
m Don't worry. If you're not sure, don't buy them.
n If the weather's good, we could have a barbecue.
o Sure. I'll get two books of first-class stamps.
p And I'll do hamburgers and steaks.

3 Useful tips

Complete the sentences with some advice!

Example
If you have hiccups,
... *hold your breath for twenty seconds.*
... *you should try sipping water slowly.*

a If you have a nosebleed, _____

_____

b If you spill red wine on a carpet, _____

_____

c If you get dandruff, _____

_____

d If you have a hangover, _____

_____

e If you can't get to sleep, _____

_____

f If you can't stop biting your nails, _____

_____

4 Combining sentences

Combine the pairs of sentences using the words in brackets. Remember that the verb form in the time clause is usually Present Simple.

Example
I'll pay you back. I'll get some money. (as soon as)
I'll pay you back as soon as I get some money.

a I want to speak to you. You're going out. (before)

_____

b I'm going to read a lot of books. We'll be away on holiday. (while)

_____

c I'll get in touch. I'll get back. (as soon as)

_____

d Would you like a cup of tea? You're going to work. (before)

_____

e I'll tell you all our news. I'll see you. (when)

_____

f I won't speak to her. She'll say sorry. (until)

_____

g Let's phone Jack now. It'll be too late. (before)

_____

h Don't go without me. Wait. I'll be ready. (until)

_____

i I'll give you a ring. We'll get back from holiday. (after)

_____

j Can you feed the cats? We'll be away on holiday. (while)

_____

Conditionals (2) and *would*

5 Sentence completion

T.46 Make second conditional sentences for the following situations.

Example
I can't give you a lift because I haven't got a car.
If I had a car, I could give you a lift.

a We won't have a holiday because we haven't got any money.

_____

b I don't know the answer, so I can't tell you.

_____

c There aren't any eggs, so I won't make an omelette.

_____

d We have three children, so we won't take a year off and travel the world.

_____

e I'm not very clever, so I won't be a doctor.

_____

f He spends all his money gambling. He isn't a wealthy man.

_____

g I haven't got any spare time. I won't learn Russian.

_____

h Jim works very hard. He has no time to spend with his family.

_____

i I've got a headache. I can't go swimming.

_____

j We haven't got a big house. We can't invite friends to stay.

_____

6 First or second conditional?

Put the verbs in brackets in the correct tense to form either a first or a second conditional clause.

a If it _____ (rain) this weekend, we _____ (not be able) to play tennis.

b Give me Peter's letter. If I _____ (see) him, I _____ (give) it to him.

c I have to work about 80 hours a week, so I'm very busy. But if I _____ (have) any spare time, I _____ (take up) a sport like golf.

d If I _____ (be) taller, I _____ (can) be a policeman, but I'm too short.

e Please start your meal. If you _____ (not have) your soup now, it _____ (go) cold.

f What noisy neighbours you've got! If my neighbours _____ (be) as bad as yours, I _____ (go) crazy.

g If you _____ (have) any problems, let me know and I _____ (come) and help you straight away.

h You're a brilliant cook! If I _____ (can) cook as well as you, I _____ (open) a restaurant.

i If there _____ (be) some nice fish in the supermarket, _____ you _____ (buy) some for supper?

j 'We have mice in the kitchen.'
   'If you _____ (have) a cat, the mice _____ soon _____ (disappear).'

7 Correcting mistakes

Correct the mistakes in the following sentences.

a I'll make some tea when everyone will arrive.
b If I'll see Peter, I'll tell him to phone you.
c If you don't be careful, you'll lose your money.
d When I'll go back to my country, I'll write to you.
e If I could travel round the world, I'll go to Hawaii.
f If you would come from my country, you would understand what I'm saying.

8 *I'd rather ...*

Say what you *would rather* do in the following situations.

Example
If you're thirsty, would you rather have a hot drink or a cold drink?
I'd rather have a cold drink.

a If you could choose between travelling by plane or by train, which would you rather do?

_____

b If you had to choose between a summer holiday or a winter holiday, which would you choose?

_____

c You have to choose between fizzy mineral water or still mineral water.

_____

d What do you want to watch on TV, the news or the football match?

_____

e In a restaurant, you have to choose between boiled potatoes or French fries.

_____

wish and *If only*

9 Wishing about the present and the past

Read the tables which show how we express wishes and regrets about the present and the past.

> ⚠️ Wishes are *unreal* and *hypothetical*.
> We use the past tense to express the unreality.

Present facts	Wishes about the present
I'm small.	*I wish I **wasn't** small.* *If only I **were** taller.*
We live in the city.	*We wish we **lived** in the country.* *If only we **didn't live** in the city!*
I'm not having a holiday this year.	*I wish I **was having** a holiday.*
I'm going to the dentist tomorrow.	*I wish I **wasn't going** to the dentist.*
I can't ski.	*I wish I **could** ski.*
John won't come to my party.	*If only he **would** come!*

> ⚠️ We express wishes and hypotheses about past facts and events by moving back one tense and using the Past Perfect. This shows the unreality and impossibility of the wish.

Past facts	Wishes about the past
I wasn't happy at school.	*I wish I **had been** happy.* *If only I'd **gone** to a different school!*
It rained the whole of my holiday.	*I wish it **hadn't rained**.* *If only it **had been** warm and sunny!*
He didn't pass his driving test.	*He wishes he'd **passed** it.*
He failed his driving test.	*He wishes he **hadn't failed**.*
I haven't been to Australia.	*I wish I'd **been** to Australia.*
Bobby's broken my vase.	*If only he **hadn't broken** it!*

What is the fact behind the following wishes?

> Example
> I wish the streets weren't so dirty.
> *The streets are very dirty.*

a I wish I wasn't out of work.

_____

b I wish there was something good on TV tonight.

_____

c I wish I didn't like chocolate so much.

_____

d If only I could lose weight!

_____

e I wish I'd won the lottery.

_____

f I wish I hadn't left school at sixteen.

_____

g If only I'd gone to university!

_____

h I wish my girlfriend had rung me last night.

_____

10 A life of regrets

T.47 Betty Arnold won nearly £10 million pounds.
Complete her regrets.

Winning the lottery was the worst thing that ever happened to me. I wish I (a) _____ . I gave my husband £5 million and he ran away with my best friend. I wish I (b) _____ _____ . The police can't find them. If only they (c) _____ . My children have changed. They are always asking me for money, and they won't do their school work. I wish they (d) _____ . I left my job at the factory which was a bad mistake. If only I (e) _____ I wouldn't have lost all my friends. I bought a big, new house in an expensive part of town but I can't find any friends here and I'm so lonely. I wish I (f) _____ . My life is miserable. My only friend is my psychiatrist. I have to see him every day and he charges £100 an hour! I wish I (g) _____ _____ .

11 Money

1 All the words in the list are to do with money. Divide them into three groups. Use your dictionary to help if necessary. Some of the words can go into more than one category.

currency	wealthy	safe	broke
accountant	bankrupt	waste	win
millionaire	economy	earn	save
cash dispenser	well-off	loan	will
stockbroker	credit card	salary	bet
penniless	economic	invest	coins
spending spree	hard up	wages	cashier
economical	squander	savings	

Nouns	Verbs	Adjectives

2 Underline the most suitable word in the sentences.

a I'm *bankrupt/broke*. Can you lend me a fiver until the weekend?

b My aunt keeps all her money in a *cash dispenser/ safe* under her bed.

c The president said that the *economic/economical* situation was very serious.

d She has *squandered/invested* all her money in government bonds.

e Isn't the pfennig a German *coin/currency*?

f My uncle's *an accountant/a spendthrift*, he helps me look after my finances.

g I didn't *bet/win* any money at the races. I don't believe in gambling.

h He *earned/wasted* all his money betting on the horses. He died penniless.

i Alan's parents are very *hard up/well-off*, they've just bought him a sports car.

j My *salary is/wages are* paid into my bank account every month.

k If only my grandfather had left me something in his *will/savings*.

12 Ways of pronouncing -oo-

T.48 The letters *-oo-* are pronounced in different ways.

Examples
soon = /uː/   book = /ʊ/   flood = /ʌ/

Say the following sentences to yourself and write all the *-oo-* words in the correct columns.

a Have you read the 'Good Food Guide' to Britain?

b The best cooks use a wooden spoon to stir the sauce.

c Look! There's a pool of blood on the carpet!

d If I won the football pools, I'd be flooded with begging letters.

e We foolishly booked a hotel room without an ensuite bathroom.

f I took my woollen jumper in case the weather turned cool in the afternoon.

g He stood on a stool and climbed onto the roof.

soon = /uː/	book = /ʊ/	flood = /ʌ/

13 Ways of pronouncing -ou-

T.49 The letters *-ou-* are also pronounced in many different ways.

Examples
four = /ɔː/   group = /uː/

1 The following groups of four words are all spelt with *-ou-*. Underline the word with the different pronunciation.

a	your	court	neighbour	pour
b	would	should	shoulder	could
c	accountant	country	count	fountain
d	drought	ought	bought	thought
e	enough	cough	rough	tough
f	anonymous	mouse	enormous	furious
g	trouble	double	doubt	country
h	through	group	soup	though

2 **T.50** Transcribe the words in phonetic script in the following sentences.

a It's the /θɔ:t/ _____ that /kaʊnts/ _____ .

b There's an /ɪˈnɔ:məs/ _____

/maʊs/ _____ in the kitchen.

c I have a lot of /ˈtrʌbl/ _____ with noisy

/ˈneɪbəz/ _____ .

d You /ɔ:t/ _____ to do something about that

/kɒf/ _____ .

e I have no /daʊt/ _____ that my boss will be

/ˈfjʊərɪəs/ _____ .

f /ɔ:lˈðəʊ/ _____ it rained last night,

we still have a /draʊt/ _____ .

Multi-word verbs

14 Multi-word verbs with more than one meaning

Many multi-word verbs have more than one meaning.

Examples
I don't *get on with* my parents.
(= don't have a good relationship with)
Don't look out the window! *Get on with* your work!
(= continue with)

Rewrite the following sentences using a multi-word verb from the box in place of the words in *italics*. Each multi-word verb is used twice with a different meaning.

| make up get over hang on work out put off go on |

a I'm trying to *calculate* how much you owe me.

_____ .

b 'Can I speak to Martin?'
'*Wait a moment*. I'll go and get him.'

_____ .

c Do you want to come with me or not? You've got to *decide*.

_____ your mind.

d Can you hear all that noise outside? I wonder what's *happening*.

_____ .

e *Hold on tight!* We're going to crash into the car in front!

_____ .

f Can we *postpone* our meeting until next week? Something urgent has come up.

_____ .

g How are we going to *climb over* the wall?

_____ .

h Is that a true story, or did you *invent* it?

_____ .

i It's one of those books where it's difficult to *understand* who all the characters are.

_____ .

j The kitchen in the restaurant was so dirty. It *made* me *not want* to eat there again.

_____ .

k Roger will never *recover from* the death of his mother.

_____ .

l 'Are you listening to me?'
'Yes, *continue speaking*. I'm listening to every word.'

_____ .

Yes, … I'm listening to every word.

THE DAILY SNOOZE

9 Modal verbs of probability
Continuous infinitive

Modal verbs of probability in the present

1 Matching

Match a line in column **A** with a line in column **B**.

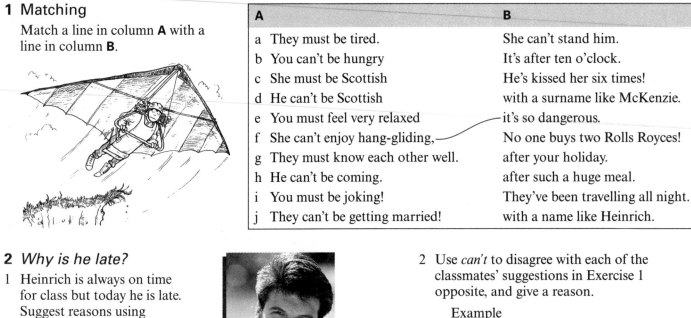

A	B
a They must be tired.	She can't stand him.
b You can't be hungry	It's after ten o'clock.
c She must be Scottish	He's kissed her six times!
d He can't be Scottish	with a surname like McKenzie.
e You must feel very relaxed	it's so dangerous.
f She can't enjoy hang-gliding,	No one buys two Rolls Royces!
g They must know each other well.	after your holiday.
h He can't be coming.	after such a huge meal.
i You must be joking!	They've been travelling all night.
j They can't be getting married!	with a name like Heinrich.

2 Why is he late?

1 Heinrich is always on time for class but today he is late. Suggest reasons using *must, might, could, may*.

> Example
> Is he still asleep ? (might)
> *He might still be asleep.*

a Is he ill? (must)

_____ .

b Is he in the coffee bar? (might)

_____ .

c Does he have a dental appointment? (could)

_____ .

d Is he stuck in a traffic jam? (may)

_____ .

e Is his train late? (might)

_____ .

f Does he want to miss the test? (must)

_____ .

2 Use *can't* to disagree with each of the classmates' suggestions in Exercise 1 opposite, and give a reason.

> Example
> *He can't still be asleep because he always gets up very early.*

a _____

_____ .

b _____

_____ .

c _____

_____ .

d _____

_____ .

e _____

_____ .

f _____

_____ .

3 Continuous infinitives

> ⚠
> 1 The continuous infinitive is used after a modal verb of probability to express a possible activity in progress at the moment.
>
> > *His light's on. He must **be working** late.*
> > *It's only 9.10. They can't **be having** a break yet.*
>
> 2 Compare the following sentences:
>
> > *John's in the garden. He**'s cutting** the grass.*
> > (I know that is what he is doing now.)
> >
> > *John's in the garden. He **must be cutting** the grass.* (I think that is what he is doing.)
> >
> > *John's garden is so beautiful. He **must cut** the grass regularly.* (I think he cuts the grass regularly.)

T.51   Complete the conversations with suitable verbs in the continuous infinitive.

Example
'Do you know where Tom is?'
'I'm not sure. He may *be playing* tennis.'

a **A** Where's Hannah?
  B She's upstairs. She must _____ her homework in her room.
  A She's not in her room.
  B Try the bathroom. She might _____ a shower.

b **A** Look over there! It's Anna and Paul.
  B She can't _____ his hand. She doesn't like him.
  A They're kissing!
  B I don't believe it! They must _____ out together.

c **A** I can't find the thing that changes the TV channel.
  B Stand up. You could _____ on it.
  A No. It's not there.

d **A** Have you seen my hair dryer?
  B Well, Ellie's just washed her hair, she may _____ it.
  A Oh! She's always washing her hair!

e **A** What's that noise?
  B It sounds like a pneumatic drill. They must _____ up the road outside.
  A What for?
  B I don't know. They could _____ for a gas leak. Our next door neighbour said she smelt gas outside her house last week.
  A No, they can't _____ for a gas leak. There's a big television van there, perhaps they're laying wires for cable TV.

Modal verbs of probability in the past

4 *must have ..., might have ..., may have ...*

Look at the scenes in the pictures and write what *must have happened* or *might have happened*. Write one or more sentences for each scene.

a *He must have locked himself out. He might have lost his key.*

b _____

  _____

c _____

  _____

d _____

  _____

e _____

  _____

f _____

  _____

g _____

  _____

h _____

  _____

5 Changing sentences

1 Rewrite the following sentences using the modal verb in brackets.

Example
I'm sure she's had a holiday. (must)
She must have had a holiday.

a I'm sure you didn't work hard for your exams. (can't)

_____

b I think they've gone to Paris. (could)

_____

c Perhaps I left my umbrella on the train. (might)

_____

d I'm sure he hasn't bought another new car. (can't)

_____

e She has probably been on a diet. (must)

_____

f It's possible that they got married in secret. (could)

_____

g I'm sure I haven't won the lottery. (can't)

_____

h Perhaps he called while we were out. (may)

_____

2 Add a reason to each of the sentences in Exercise 1.

Example
*She must have had a holiday **because** she's very brown.*

6 A poem

1 **T.52** Read the poem opposite.

2 What has happened in the poem? Put a tick (✔) if you think the sentence is possible, and a cross (✘) if you think it isn't possible. If you're not sure, put (**?**).

a ☐ He must have left her.
   ☐ She must have left him.
b ☐ They can't have been husband and wife.
   ☐ They definitely lived together.
c ☐ They must have been together for a long time.
   ☐ They can't have been together for a long time.
d ☐ He might be glad she's gone.
   ☐ He must be missing her very much.
e ☐ The house must seem very quiet.
   ☐ He might have pets to keep him company.
f ☐ He must have done something to upset her.

The house is not the same since you left

The house is not the same since you left
the cooker is angry – it blames me
The TV tries desperately to stay busy
but occasionally I catch it staring out of the window
The washing-up's feeling sorry for itself again
it just sits there saying
'What's the point, what's the point?'
The curtains count the days
Nothing in the house will talk to me
I think your armchair's dead
The kettle tried to comfort me at first
but you know what its attention span is like
I've not told the plants yet
they think you're still on holiday
The bathroom misses you
I hardly see it these days
It still can't believe you didn't take it with you
The bedroom won't even look at me
since you left it keeps its eyes closed
all it wants to do is sleep, remembering better times
trying to lose itself in dreams
it seems like it's taken the easy way out
but at night I hear the pillows
weeping into the sheets.

Henry Normal

☐ She has definitely done something to upset him.
g ☐ He can't be using the bathroom much.
   ☐ He might be trying to avoid using the bathroom.
h ☐ She must have spent a lot of time in the bathroom.
   ☐ The bathroom might have been her favourite room.
i ☐ He might be sleeping downstairs.
   ☐ He can't be sleeping in their old bedroom.

Vocabulary

7 Verbs and nouns that go together

1 Put a verb from the box next to the nouns.
There are two noun phrases for each verb.

wipe	pour	chop	crush	squeeze
plant	pick	twist	rub	tear /tɜə/

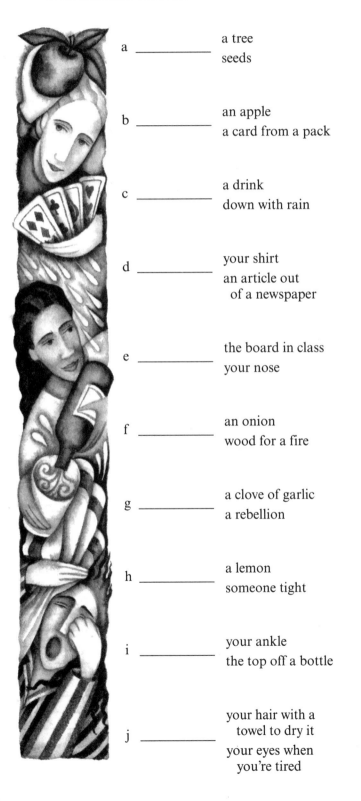

a _____   a tree
              seeds

b _____   an apple
              a card from a pack

c _____   a drink
              down with rain

d _____   your shirt
              an article out
                of a newspaper

e _____   the board in class
              your nose

f _____   an onion
              wood for a fire

g _____   a clove of garlic
              a rebellion

h _____   a lemon
              someone tight

i _____   your ankle
              the top off a bottle

j _____   your hair with a
                towel to dry it
              your eyes when
                you're tired

2 Choose the best answer.

a (In a crowded train) 'Excuse me! Can I just _____
  past? Thank you.'
   1 twist   2 crush   3 squeeze

b Someone has spilled water on the floor. I'll have to
  _____ it up.
   1 pour   2 wipe   3 pick

c He thought his cheque had come. He _____ open
  the envelope, but it was just a bill.
   1 tore   2 twisted   3 chopped

d There were twenty people in the lift. I was nearly
  _____ to death!
   1 torn   2 crushed   3 rubbed

e We _____ the tomatoes when they were ripe.
   1 squeezed   2 planted   3 picked

f I tried to _____ the last bit of toothpaste
  out of the tube.
   1 squeeze   2 twist   3 crush

g 'How do I get the top off this lemonade bottle?'
  '_____ it.'
   1 rub   2 tear   3 twist

h (To a butcher) 'Could you _____ the chicken into
  eight pieces, please?'
   1 tear   2 chop   3 twist

i 'Have a drink,' he said, _____ me a glass
  of red wine.
   1 pouring   2 wiping   3 planting

j Peter was _____ his knee where he
  had fallen over and bruised it.
   1 squeezing   2 rubbing   3 picking

k Where do you want to _____ this lovely apple tree?
   1 plant   2 chop   3 twist

l 'Can I borrow one of your books?'
  'Sure. _____ any one you want.'
   1 plant   2 pick   3 tear

m 'What have you done to your fingers?'
  'I _____ them in a door. The door slammed
  closed in the wind, and my fingers were in it.'
   1 crushed   2 twisted   3 squeezed

n Most people, when they get a spot on their face, have to
  _____ it.
   1 wipe   2 tear   3 squeeze

o She was angry. She got the letter and _____ it in
  half, then threw it away.
   1 tore   2 crushed   3 twisted

Pronunciation

8 Connected speech

> **T.53** Look at the examples which show how words link together in spoken English.
>
> *He must have eaten all Ann's oranges.*
> /hi məst‿əv‿iːtən ɔːl‿ænz‿ɒrɪndʒɪz/
>
> *She can't have asked Al's aunt.*
> /ʃi kɑːnt‿əv‿ɑːskt‿ælz‿ɑːnt/

T.54 Say aloud the phonetic transcriptions of the following sentences. Then transcribe the sentences and mark the linked words.

Examples
/ʃi məst‿əv‿iːtən ðə tʃiːz/
She must have eaten the cheese.

/juː kɑːnt‿əv‿siːn‿ɪm/
You can't have seen him.

a /hi kɑːnt əv əraɪvd ɜːlɪ/

_____

b /juː məst əv bɪn ɪn æfrɪkə/

_____

c /ðeɪ məs bi kʌmɪŋ suːn/

_____

d /ʃi maɪt əv bɪn æŋgrɪ/

_____

e /hi kʊd əv gɒn əbrɔːd/

_____

f /ʃi meɪ bi əraɪvɪŋ ðɪs ɑːftənuːn/

_____

g /ðeɪ kɑːnt əv bɪn ɪn lʌv/

_____

h /ðeɪ maɪt əv iːtən ɪt ɔːl/

_____

9 Shifting stress

T.55 Say aloud **B**'s sentences, then mark the change in main stress each time.

a **A** Mr Harper must have left the black bag in the taxi.
   B Did you say Mr Harper must have left the blue bag in the taxi?

b **A** Mr Harper must have left the black bag in the taxi.
   B Did you say Mr Harper must have left the black suitcase in the taxi?

c **A** Mr Harper must have left the black bag in the taxi.
   B Did you say Mrs Harper must have left the black bag in the taxi?

d **A** Mr Harper must have left the black bag in the taxi.
   B Did you say Mr Harper must have put the black bag in the taxi?

e **A** Mr Harper must have left the black bag in the taxi.
   B Did you say Mr Harper must have left the black bag in the train?

f **A** Mr Harper must have left the black bag in the taxi.
   B Did you say Mr Harper must have left a black bag in the taxi?

g **A** Mr Harper must have left the black bag in the taxi.
   B Did you say Mr Harper might have left the black bag in the taxi?

h **A** Mr Harper must have left the black bag in the taxi.
   B Did you say Mr Harper can't have left the black bag in the taxi?

10 Adjective + preposition

Many adjectives are followed by certain prepositions.
Fill each gap with a preposition from the box.

for	at	about	with	to	in	of	from

a 'What are you so excited _____ ?'
   'We're going on holiday tomorrow.'

b 'I'm very angry _____ you.'
   'Why? What have I done?'

c Are you any good _____ maths? I'm hopeless.

d Jenny's getting married _____ Harry.
   Did you know?

e We keep a light on at night because I'm afraid

   _____ the dark.

f My sister's very different _____ me. I'm blond
   but she's brunette.

g I'm tired _____ work. I want a holiday.

h I feel very sorry _____ Kathy. Five kids and a
   foul husband. What sort of life is that?

i Are you interested _____ travel programmes?
   There's one on telly tonight.

j Teenagers are often rude _____ their parents.

k I'm very proud _____ my children. I think
   they're wonderful.

l Did you know that chewing gum is good _____
   your teeth? Well, it is.

m Everyone likes Bill. He's good-looking, witty and

   charming, and I'm very jealous _____ him!

n 'I told her I thought she was stupid.'

   'That wasn't very kind _____ you.'

o I haven't heard from Len for ages. I'm a bit worried

   _____ him.

p My homework was full _____ mistakes.

q Italy is famous _____ its antiquities and
   its ice-cream.

r 'The train leaves at 10.00.'

   'Are you sure _____ that?'

s When you leave home, you're responsible _____
   everything!

t I'm fed up _____ this weather! Where's the
   sunshine gone?

Present Perfect Continuous
Continuous aspect
Time expressions

Present Perfect Continuous

1 Present Perfect Simple or Continuous?

1 T.56 Tick (✔) the box for the correct verb form.

a I've ☐ lost / ☐ been losing my passport.

Have you ☐ seen / ☐ been seeing it anywhere?

b Someone ☐ has eaten / ☐ has been eating the chocolates! They're nearly all gone!

c I've ☐ waited / ☐ been waiting for you for ages! Where have you been?

d I've ☐ crashed / ☐ been crashing your car. I'm awfully sorry.

e How many exercises ☐ have you done / ☐ have you been doing today?

f 'Why are you red?' 'I've ☐ run. / ☐ been running.'

g I have ☐ never read / ☐ never been reading a better book in my life.

h How long have you ☐ known / ☐ been knowing Ann and John?

i I've ☐ painted / ☐ been painting the living room for a week. It'll be finished soon.

j I've ☐ painted / ☐ been painting the living room. I finished last night.

k I don't know what our neighbours are doing.

They've ☐ had / ☐ been having a row all day.

l They've ☐ had / ☐ been having five rows this week.

2 Put the verb in brackets in the correct tense, Present Perfect Simple or Continuous.

a I'm exhausted! I _____ (work) all day, and I _____ (not finish) yet.

b I _____ (visit) many countries over the past few years.

c Someone _____ (take) my books.

I _____ (look) for them for ages, but

I _____ (not find) them yet.

d I _____ (shop) all morning, but

I _____ (not buy) anything.

e That's one of the best books I _____

ever _____ (read).

f 'You're filthy! What _____ you

_____ (do)?'

'I _____ (work) in the garden.'

g The streets are all wet. It _____ (rain).

h I _____ (listen) to you for the past half an hour, but I'm afraid I _____ (not understand) a single word.

i 'What's the matter?'

'I _____ (read) in my room for hours, and I've got a headache.'

j I _____ (try) to lose weight for ages.

I _____ (lose) ten pounds so far.

k 'Why is your hair wet?'

'I _____ (swim).'

2 Questions

Make questions using the prompts.

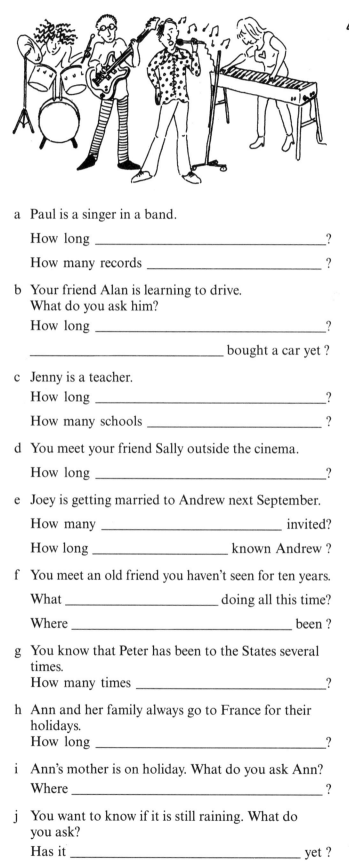

a Paul is a singer in a band.

How long _____?

How many records _____ ?

b Your friend Alan is learning to drive.
What do you ask him?

How long _____?

_____ bought a car yet ?

c Jenny is a teacher.

How long _____?

How many schools _____ ?

d You meet your friend Sally outside the cinema.

How long _____?

e Joey is getting married to Andrew next September.

How many _____ invited?

How long _____ known Andrew ?

f You meet an old friend you haven't seen for ten years.

What _____ doing all this time?

Where _____ been ?

g You know that Peter has been to the States several times.
How many times _____?

h Ann and her family always go to France for their holidays.
How long _____?

i Ann's mother is on holiday. What do you ask Ann?
Where _____ ?

j You want to know if it is still raining. What do you ask?
Has it _____ yet ?

Continuous aspect

⚠️

1 Verb forms in the simple aspect see actions as a complete whole. Verb forms in the continuous aspect see activities in progress. The activities have duration, a beginning and an end.

*An astronomer **studies** the stars.*
*I'm **studying** modern languages at university.*

2 The continuous has the effect of lengthening an activity. It has duration, and it can be interrupted. Other events can happen in the middle of it.

*When I woke up this morning, it **was raining**.*
 (= interrupted activity)

The simple aspect expresses 'simple' actions.
*It **rained** every day during our holidays.*
 (= simple fact)

*I **watch** TV every night.*
*Ssh! Don't interrupt me while I'm **watching** the news.*

3 Because the continuous can express interrupted activities, the activities might not be completed.

*Who's **eaten** my sandwich?*
*Who's **been eating** my sandwich?*

*He **died**. There was nothing we could do.*
*He **was dying**, but the doctors managed to resuscitate him.*

4 The continuous can also express the idea of limited duration. The activity does not last forever, it has a beginning and an end.

*I **go** to work by train.*
*I'm **going** to work by car this week because there's a train strike.*

*He **works** in a bank. (= his permanent occupation)*
*She's **working** on a farm during the holidays.*
 (= a temporary job)

We cannot say a sentence such as **The apple tree was standing in the middle of the courtyard*, because the use of the continuous suggests a temporary situation – at other times the apple tree stood somewhere else!

3 Matching

T.57 Match a line in **A** with a line in **B**. Write **1** or **2** in the box.

A		B
a ☐ I drive to work.		1 There's a train strike.
b ☐ I'm driving to work today.		2 It usually takes about twenty-five minutes.
c **1** I think		1 you're beautiful.
d **2** I'm thinking		2 of buying a flat in London.
e ☐ He might study		1 French when he goes to university.
f ☐ He might be studying		2 in his room. The light's on.
g ☐ She has		1 a good time in Spain.
h ☐ She's having		2 a good job.
i ☐ She cut		1 her finger and it bled a lot.
j ☐ She was cutting		2 the grass when I arrived.
k ☐ She must be washing		1 her hair. I can hear the shower going.
l ☐ She must wash		2 her hair at least three times a week.
m ☐ I've smoked		1 too many cigarettes today.
n ☐ I've been smoking		2 since I was sixteen.
o ☐ Anna's gone		1 out with Phil for ages.
p ☐ Anna's been going		2 to China for a few months.

> I think you're beautiful.

> I'm thinking of buying a flat in London.

4 Simple or Continuous?

Put the verb in brackets in either the simple or the continuous.
Look at the reference at the end of the sentence to help you decide what tense or verb form to use.

Example
I _____ (work) when Helen _____ (phone).   Past
I was working when Helen phoned.

a Helen _____ (come) from Sheffield.
Present (all time)

b She _____ (come) to see me this evening.   Future arrangement

c She _____ (work) in a bank.
Present (all time)

d She _____ (work) for the same bank for a year.   Present Perfect

e She _____ (have) the same boss for six months.   Present Perfect

f She _____ (have) a row with him yesterday.   Past

g So now Helen _____ (want) to change her job.   Present

h She _____ (think) of working abroad.   Present

i Her parents _____ (think) this is a good idea.   Present

j She'd like _____ (find) a job in the tourist industry.   Infinitive

k She should _____ (work) now, but she isn't. She's daydreaming.   Infinitive

l She _____ (go) to bed very late last night.   Past

m When she _____ (wake) up this morning, it _____ (rain).   Past

n She _____ (take) some aspirin now because she _____ (have) a headache.   Present

o She wants _____ (go) home.
Infinitive

p If she were at home, she would _____ (sit) in her kitchen having a cup of coffee.   Infinitive

Time expressions

5 When Sally met Harry

Look at the charts of life events for Harry and Sally.
Complete the questions and answers.

Harry

age	
0	Born 1970
11	Went to Loughborough Grammar School for 6 years
18	Went to London University for 3 years
19	Started going out with Suzie Ended Christmas 1993
22	Went to live in Paris Feb–July 1992
23	Met Sally at a party
24	Got a job in a record shop
25	Married Sally 23 March 1995 Promoted to store manager of the record shop Autumn 1995
26	Bought a house in Wimbledon

now

Sally

age	
0	Born 1967 in Ontario, Canada
11	Joined a drama group Start of a life-long passion
15	Came to live in England summer 1982
19	Went to Teacher Training College for 3 years
23	Taught in Poland for two years
24	Met and married Paul August 1991 Had a daughter, Polly, born 13 May 1992
25	Came back to England with Polly but without Paul 1992
26	Divorced Paul Started teaching in a school in London Sept 1993 Met Harry Christmas 1993

now

a When _____ ?
   In 1970.

b How long _____ at Loughborough
   Grammar School?
   Until _____ .

c How long _____ ?
   Three years.

d How long _____ Suzie?

   _____

e How long _____ in Paris?

   _____

f Where _____ ?
   At a party.

g How long _____
   in the record shop?

   _____

h How long _____ manager?
   Since _____ .

i When _____ ?
   ___ 23 March 1995.

j How long _____ they
   _____ in Wimbledon?
   Since _____ .

k How long _____ Sally
   _____ in Canada?
   _____ she was fifteen.

l How long _____
   interested in drama?
   _____ she was 11.

m When _____ meet Paul?
   While _____ .

n When _____
   married for the first time?

   _____

o When _____ Polly _____ ?

   _____

p How long _____
   married to Paul?

   _____

q How long _____
   married to Harry?

   _____

r How long _____
   in the school in London?
   Since _____ .

s When _____ meet Harry?
   _____ Christmas time in 1993.

6 Suffixes and prefixes

1 Make at least *one* new word with each base word using either a suffix or a prefix. Use your dictionary to help. Sometimes you will need to change the spelling a little.

Prefix	Base word	Suffix
	possible	
	thought	
	agree	
	care	
	hope	
un	conscious	ful
in	human	less
	success	
im	polite	able
il	help	ness
	understand	
dis	taste	ment
mis	legal	ity
	logical	
	stress	
	popular	
	use	
	like	

a <u>impossible   possibility</u>

b _____

c _____

d _____

e _____

f _____

g _____

h _____

i _____

j _____

k _____

l _____

m _____

n _____

o _____

p _____

q _____

r _____

2 Complete the sentences with the correct form of the word in brackets.

a The situation was _____ . Nobody could do anything to help. (hope)

b He was _____ for three days after the accident. (conscious)

c Rudeness never gets you what you want. _____ always pays! (polite)

d The conditions in the men's prison were _____ . (human)

e My husband and I usually get on really well; the only thing we ever have any _____ about is money. (agree)

f He's a bully. That's why he's so _____ with his school friends. (popular)

g Don't _____ me. I really want to come to your party but I can't. (understand)

h Thank you very much. You've been very _____ . (help)

i She's a very sweet child. Very _____ indeed, not at all _____ like her sister. (like) (polite)

j I can't follow you. What you're saying is totally _____ . (logical)

k I'm very _____ about what I eat, and I've been doing exercises for weeks, but it's all totally _____ . I haven't lost any weight! (care) (use)

l He caused her so much _____ with that _____ comment about how awful she looked on her wedding day. (stress) (thought)

7 Prepositions of time

Put the correct preposition of time into each gap.

Young Beethoven (1770–1827)

a Beethoven began his musical education _____ the age of five.

b I lived in Paris _____ five years, _____ 1975 _____ 1980.

c We never see our cat. _____ the day it sleeps, and it goes out _____ night.

d I don't usually go out _____ the evening, except _____ Monday evening, when I play snooker.

e Generations of my family have lived in this house _____ 1800.

f 'How long are you in England for?'
' _____ six months.'

g 'How much longer are you staying?'
' _____ the end of the month.
Then I have to go home.'

h I'm just going out to the shops. If anyone rings, tell then I'll be back _____ a few minutes.

i Are you going away _____ Easter?

j I met my husband in Wales. _____ the time I was working in a pub.

8 Diphthongs

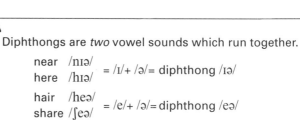

Diphthongs are *two* vowel sounds which run together.

near /nɪə/
here /hɪə/ = /ɪ/ + /ə/ = diphthong /ɪə/

hair /heə/
share /ʃeə/ = /e/ + /ə/ = diphthong /eə/

1 **T.58** Write the words from the box next to the correct diphthong. There are two more words for each diphthong.

where	clear	stay	shy	beer	weigh
know	sure	now	noise	phone	bear
high	enjoy	aloud	poor		

a /ɪ/ + /ə/ = /ɪə/ near _____ _____

b /e/ + /ə/ = /eə/ hair _____ _____

c /e/ + /ɪ/ = /eɪ/ pay _____ _____

d /ə/ + /ʊ/ = /əʊ/ go _____ _____

e /a/ + /ɪ/ = /aɪ/ my _____ _____

f /ɔː/ + /ɪ/ = /ɔɪ/ boy _____ _____

g /a/ + /ʊ/ = /aʊ/ how _____ _____

h /ʊ/ + /ə/ = /ʊə/ tour* _____ _____

*Some native speakers do not use the diphthong /ʊə/. They use /ɔː/ and say /tɔː/ for *tour*. However, this is becoming less frequent.

2 **T.59** Transcribe the words in the sentences in phonetic script. They are all diphthongs.

a We caught the /pleɪn/ _____ to the /saʊθ/ _____ of /speɪn/ _____ .

b The /bɔɪ/ _____ in the red /kəʊt/ _____ said that he /ɪnˈdʒɔɪd/ _____ the journey.

c I've /nəʊn/ _____ Sally for /ˈnɪəlɪ/ _____ /faɪv/ _____ years.

d She's /ˈweərɪŋ/ _____ a red /rəʊz/ _____ in her /heə/ _____ .

e Fewer people /sməʊk/ _____ /paɪps/ _____ these /deɪz/ _____ .

f He /laɪks/ _____ to /raɪd/ _____ a big black /ˈməʊtəbaɪk/ _____ .

Indirect questions
Questions with a preposition at the end
Question tags

Indirect questions

1 Yes/No questions

1 **T.60** Write in the correct form of the auxiliary verbs *do*, *be*, or *have* to complete the questions in Quiz 1.

QUIZ 1

a _____ the town of Timbuktu in Africa?

b _____ all birds lay eggs?

c _____ dinosaurs lay eggs?

d _____ John F. Kennedy the youngest American president?

e _____ there ever been a female president of the USA?

f _____ the Olympic Games ever been held in the same city more than once?

g _____ Switzerland have a president?

h _____ William Shakespeare ever live in London?

2 Which questions can you answer?
Write in the answers if you can. If you don't know the answer, write what is most true for you.

> *I don't know if …*   *I've no idea if …*
> *I (don't) think …*   *I'm not sure if …*
> *I can't remember if …*

a *I've no idea if Timbuktu is in Africa.*

b _____

c _____

d _____

e _____

f _____

g _____

h _____

2 Wh-questions

1 **T.61** Write in the correct question word *What*, *When*, *Where*, *Who*, or *Which* to complete Quiz 2.

QUIZ 2

a _____ does the word 'alphabet' come from?

b _____ kind of weather does the Beaufort Scale measure?

c _____ European countries does the Danube flow through?

d _____ was the first man in space?

e _____ does NASA stand for?

f _____ did Adolph Hitler marry?

g _____ did Margaret Thatcher become Prime Minister of Britain?

h _____ Latin American country did Montezuma II rule in the 16th century?

2 Which questions can you answer? Write in the answers if you can. If you don't know the answer, write what is most true for you.

> *I don't know …*   *I've no idea …*
> *I'm not sure …*   *I can't remember …*

a _____

b _____

c _____

d _____

e _____

f _____

g _____

h _____

3 Do you know where ...?

Complete the sentences.

Example
A Where's the bank?
B I'm afraid I don't know _where the bank is_.

a **A** Could you tell me what _____ ?
   B It's nearly half past six.

b **A** Where have I put my glasses?
   B You're always forgetting _____ !

c **A** What are you giving your children for Christmas?
   B We haven't decided _____ yet.

d **A** Did you post my letter?
   B I can't remember _____ or not.

e **A** Whose pen is this?
   B I've no idea _____ .

f **A** Are you coming on the boat trip?
   B I'm not sure _____ .

g **A** Do you know _____ Carol White _____ ?
   B Yes, she's the girl with the blonde hair, talking to Bob.

h **A** How much does Jack weigh?
   B I haven't a clue _____ .

i **A** Where does David get all his money from?
   B No idea, but I'd love to know _____ .

j **A** Have you any idea how much _____ on clothes?
   B I don't want to know how much I spend. I don't care.

4 Newspaper headlines

Put the words in the right order to make indirect questions about the newspaper headlines.

Example

Man wins record amount on Lottery

he'll   away   wonder   give   I   if   any
I wonder if he'll give any away.

Oldest man in the world celebrates birthday

a   is   don't   how   he   we   know   old   exactly

_____

b   birthday   celebrate   wonder   going   I   how
    he's   his   to

_____

BANK ROBBER ESCAPES FROM PRISON

c   managed   how   get   nobody   out   he   knows
    to

_____

d   helped   escape   wonder   who   I   to   him

_____

Actress marries husband number 7

e   know   didn't   she'd   many   I   been   so   times
    married

_____

f   went   wonder   I   wrong   last   with   marriage
    what   her

_____

SHOCK DEFEAT FOR ITALIAN FOOTBALL TEAM

g   know   what   like   to   the   I'd   score   was

_____

h   doesn't   headline   the   say   were   they   against
    playing   who

_____

British man arrested at Bangkok Airport

i   wonder   where   I   going   fly   to   he   was   to

_____

j   wonder   I   he   smuggle   if   to   drugs   trying
    was

_____

5 Visiting a town

1 **T.62** Read about Sydney, Australia.

Sydney

Sydney has a population of **(a)** __ . It is Australia's largest and oldest city, and it is built around the harbour, named **(b)** __ . Captain Cook called it this when he sailed to the area in **(c)** __ .

Sydney wasn't planned from the start, as many later Australian cities were. It has a tight, congested centre without wide boulevards. But it is a very **(d)** __ city, with the most energy and style of all Australian cities.

In Sydney, the buildings are higher, the colours are brighter and the nightlife more exciting. North of the harbour is more residential, and the south is more industrial. The two shores are joined by the Sydney Harbour Bridge, which was built in **(e)** __ . The city centre is **(f)** __ .

Sydney's most famous building, the Opera House, was opened in **(g)** __ . Designed in the 1950s by a young Danish architect, **(h)** __ , it is supposed to look like sails in the wind. It took 16 years to build.

The best place to go shopping is **(i)** __ . The Post Office is **(j)** __ .

The climate in New South Wales is **(k)** __ . There are some of the best beaches in the world, notably Bondi Beach and Manly.

Tourist offices are open five days a week from **(l)** __ to 5 pm.

2 Complete the indirect questions about Sydney.

a Do you know what _____ ?

b I've no idea what _____ .

c I wonder when _____ .

d I wonder what sort _____ .

e Do you know when _____ ?

f Could you tell me where _____ ?

g I've no idea when _____ .

h I haven't a clue who _____ .

i Could you tell me where _____ ?

j Do you know where _____ ?

k I wonder what _____ like.

l Do you happen to know what _____ ?

3 Here are the answers to the questions!
   Put a letter a–1 next to each one.

1 ☐ It is a very modern city.

2 ☐ 1770.

3 ☐ Joern Utzon.

4 ☐ 9 am.

5 ☐ Port Jackson.

6 ☐ It is generally warm, though it can get a little cold in winter.

7 ☐ It is on Martin Place.

8 ☐ The best place is George Street and Pitt Street.

9 ☐ 3,700,000

10 ☐ 1932.

11 ☐ 1973.

12 ☐ It is south of the harbour.

Questions with a preposition at the end

6 Who did you speak to?

> ⚠️
>
> 1 Many verbs have dependent prepositions.
>
> | | | |
> |---|---|---|
> | speak **to** | talk **about** | look **for** |
> | dance **with** | think **about** | point **at** |
>
> 2 When we ask a question about the object of the sentence, the preposition usually comes at the end.
>
> *What did you talk **about**?*
> *What were you looking **for**?*
> *Who did she dance **with**?*
> *What are you pointing **at**?*
> *What are you thinking **about**?*
>
> We don't put the preposition at the beginning of the sentence. NOT *~~About what did you talk?~~*

1 Make questions from the statements, asking about the words in *italics*.

Example
Who are you looking at?
I'm looking at *that man*.

a _____ ?
I'm waiting for *the postman*.

b _____ ?
He works for *Barclays Bank*.

c _____ about?
I'm thinking about *what to cook for supper*.

d _____ ?
I stayed with *some friends*.

e _____ ?
The pen belongs to *me*.

f _____ ?
The letter is from *the Tax Office*.

g _____ ?
He died of *a heart attack*.

h _____ ?
I'm worried about *the exams*.

i _____
_____ ?
I'm staring at *the dirty mark on the end of your nose*.

j _____ ?
I'm writing to *my aunt in Australia*.

2 **T.63** We sometimes use short questions in our responses. Write short questions with a question word and a preposition.

Example
Ken's getting married.
Who to?

a Come here! I want to talk to you!

_____ ?

b Bye! I'm going.

_____ ?

c Give me a cloth! Quick!

_____ ?

d I had lunch in the Café Royal yesterday.

_____ ?

e My parents were absolutely furious with me!

_____ ?

f Ssh! I'm thinking!

_____ ?

g Don't you think you should apologize to her?

_____ ?

h You'd better hand in the purse you found.

_____ ?

i Pat and I had an argument, as usual.

_____ ?

j Eat your food.

_____ ? I haven't got a knife or fork.

Question tags

7 Complete the tag

T.64 Put a question tag at the end of the sentences.

Example
Salzburg's in Austria, _isn't it_ ?

a You don't like beefburgers, _____ ?

b You're going to France, _____ ?

c We had a good time, _____ ?

d It's hot today, _____ ?

e You can't use a word processor, _____ ?

f You won't tell anyone, _____ ?

g We don't have to go yet, _____ ?

h I'm so stupid, _____ ?

i You haven't met Jane, _____ ?

j They didn't like the film, _____ ?

8 Situations

1 T.65 Write sentences with a question tag for the following situations. Use the verb in brackets.

Example
You're in a restaurant. Your daughter is playing with her food. You can tell she isn't happy. (like)
You don't like your food, do you?

a You and your boyfriend are getting ready to go to a party. He doesn't usually like parties. He's looking pretty miserable. (want)

_____ ?

b You went to the party. Your boyfriend had a lot to drink. The next day he doesn't feel very well. (had)

_____ ?

c You're out shopping. You see a dress that is absolutely beautiful, so you try it on. What do you say to your friend? (is lovely)

_____ ?

d You're in the cinema. Your friend isn't enjoying the film because it's very violent. (enjoy)

_____ ?

e You go to a concert. It's brilliant. What do you say to your friend as you're leaving? (was superb)

_____ ?

2 T.66 Ask people to do things, or ask for information, with a sentence and a question tag.

Example
It's raining, and you need to go to the station. Pete has a car. Perhaps he could give you a lift.
Pete, you couldn't give me a lift to the station, could you?

a You're broke.
Maybe Larry could lend you five pounds.

Larry, _____ ?

b You've lost your car keys.
Perhaps Kate knows where they are.

Kate, _____ ?

c You need a Russian dictionary.
Perhaps Tricia's got one.

Tricia, _____ ?

d You're looking for Bill. Maybe Sue has seen him.

Sue, _____ ?

e You need change for a five-pound note.
Maybe the newspaper seller could change it for you.

Excuse me, you _____ ?

3 In Exercise 1, do the question tags go up or down? What about the question tags in Exercise 2?

9 Dialogues

T.67 Put in question tags where you think they are appropriate in the following dialogues.

a **A** I can't do this exercise. It's very difficult.
B Don't worry. I'm here to help you.
A I'll be able to do it if I practise.
B Of course. It took me ages to learn.

b **A** The Browns have got loads of money.
B I know. They're always going on holiday.
A I don't know where they get it from.
B Still, we're happy with what we've got.

c **A** You aren't going out dressed like that.
B Why not? I can wear what I want.
A That depends. You're wearing my jacket.
B No, I'm not. I bought this yesterday.

d **A** Dave's new car is great.
B Yes, it's lovely. But he drives much too fast.
A Yes, it's true.
B You wouldn't like one like that.
A Yes, I would. I'd give anything to have a car like that.

Vocabulary

10 Animal idioms

1 The list of idioms below all contain the names of animals. Look at the cartoons and write in the name of the animals.

a to smell a _____

f to talk until the

_____ come home

b to set the _____

amongst the _____

g to be gentle as a

_____

c to behave like a

_____ in a china shop

h to be unable to say

boo to a _____

d to sort out the _____

from the _____

i to have a

_____ party

e to make an _____

of yourself

j to be like water off

a _____'s back

2 Read the situation and complete the idiom from Exercise 1 which describes it.

a I hadn't seen my old school friends for ages, so we stayed up talking for most of the night. We talked

_____

b The test was very difficult. It showed the teacher which students had done the work and which students hadn't. It really sorted out

_____

c My brother's getting married on Saturday and he's going out with all his mates the evening before. He's having a

_____

d Our dog's very big and fierce-looking but he's very good with babies and children. He's as

_____

e I didn't believe a word that salesman said about that car. I knew he was lying about the number of miles it had done. I really smelt

_____

f It doesn't matter how much you get angry with her, it has no effect. It's like

_____

g The interview was terrible. I forgot everything I wanted to say, and I couldn't answer their questions either. I really made

_____

h Careful! You're so clumsy. You're knocking everything off the table. You're like

_____

i I didn't know that Bob knew nothing about Anna and Peter. When I told him he went white. I think I've really set

_____

j Maisie is such a shy little girl; she never puts her hand up, she can't say

_____

⚠️ It is important to be able to recognize idioms when you hear or read them, but it can be very difficult to use them naturally and successfully in conversation yourself!

Pronunciation

11 A poem

1 **T.68** Read the poem aloud to yourself. Some of the words are in phonetic script.

When did the world begin?
by Robert Clairmont

'When did the world begin and how?'
I asked /ə læm ə gəʊt ə kaʊ/.

'What's it all about and why?'
I asked /ə pɪg əz hi went baɪ/.

'Where will the whole thing end, and when?'
I asked /ə dʌk ə guːs ə hen/.

And I copied all their answers too,
/ə kwæk ə bɑː ən ɔɪŋk ə muː/.

2 Transcribe the words in phonetic script. What animal noises are there?

12 Onomatopoeic words

T.69 A word that is onomatopoeic sounds like what it means.

Example
The lion /rɔːd/ ___roared___ loudly.

Transcribe the onomatopoeic words in the following sentences.

a My husband always /snɔːz/ _____ .
   I can't get to sleep.

b Ssh! It's a secret. I'll /ˈwɪspə/ _____ it to you.

c She saw a dark shape in the night and she
   /skriːmd/ _____ but it was only the dog.

d He lay on the ground /ˈgrəʊnɪŋ/ _____
   with pain.

e There was a gust of wind and the door
   /bæŋd/ _____ shut.

f The wine glass /smæʃt/ _____ into a
   thousand pieces.

g The cat /skrætʃt/ _____ the leg of the chair.

h He walked down the road /ˈwɪslɪŋ/ _____ a
   happy tune.

Multi-word verbs

13 Common multi-word verbs

1 Look at the multi-word verbs in the box.
   Check any that you don't know in your dictionary.

take up (time)	carry on with	put up with
go on (= happen)	let sb down	set off
keep on (doing sth)	tell sb off	Come on!
fall out with sb	come across	pick sb up

2 Write in the correct multi-word verb in the right form.
   The dictionary definition is given to help you.

a There's a terrible noise outside.
   What's_____ ? (happen)

b I'm going to bed. We need to_____ at
   about 7.00 tomorrow morning so that we're at the
   airport by 8.00. (begin a journey)

c I was tidying out the attic the other day, and I
   _____ some old photographs of when I
   was a baby. (find by accident)

d My teenage daughters are driving me crazy. I can't
   _____ their moods, their music, and
   their constant demands for money. (tolerate)

e I'm going to give up tennis. I love it, but
   it_____ so much time, and I'm so busy
   at the moment. (fill or occupy)

f A teacher to the class: 'Don't stop just because a
   visitor has come to the class! _____
   your work!' (continue)

g I'll _____ you _____ at your house at 7.00
   and we'll go to the disco. Make sure you're all ready.
   (collect in a car)

h 'Why is your son crying?' 'I _____ him _____
   for playing football in the garden and smashing a
   window.' (speak angrily to sb for doing sth wrong)

i I'm relying on you to be there tomorrow to help me.
   Don't _____ me _____ . (disappoint)

j She's _____ with her boyfriend again.
   He arrived two hours late yesterday, and they had a
   huge row. (have a quarrel)

k Said by someone at a football match:
   '_____ , England! We need another
   goal!' (said to encourage sb to try harder)

l 'The door handle's broken again.' 'I know. I've
   mended it again and again, but it _____
   coming off. I don't know how to stop it.' (continue)

Reported speech
ask and *tell*
speak and *talk*

Reported statements and questions

1 An argument

Brian and Thelma have just returned from their honeymoon in Barbados. They had a terrible time and they have just had their first big argument.

1 **T.70** Read the report of the argument in Thelma's diary.

September

24 Sunday

Brian and I had our first big row last night – all about our honeymoon, of course. It was horrible! We shouted at each other!

He told me that it was my fault that we'd gone to Barbados and that it had cost a fortune and had been the worst holiday he had ever had.

I said that there was nothing wrong with Barbados, it was very beautiful, but the travel firm were to blame. Their brochure had promised all kinds of things about the hotel and it had all been lies. I told him that he had no right to blame me and I started crying.

Brian said he was sorry and that he knew that it wasn't my fault really. He said that he would go to the travel agent first thing in the morning and that he would tell them about everything that had gone wrong. I said that I would go, too, because I was going to ask for our money back or another holiday.

Let's see what happens tomorrow!!

2 **T.71** Write the actual words of their argument.

Brian It's your fault that _____

_____

_____

_____

Thelma There's _____

_____

_____

_____

Brian I'm _____

_____

_____

_____

Thelma I'll _____

_____

_____

2 But you said ...

T.72 Read the holiday brochure and complete the conversation between Brian, Thelma and the travel agent.

THE HOLIDAY OF YOUR DREAMS
The Copa D'or Hotel Barbados

Location
- You will fly there on Concorde in just two hours.
- The hotel is twenty minutes from the airport.
- It has four acres of tropical gardens.

Facilities
- Your room will have wonderful views over the sea.
- The beautiful gardens lead directly onto the beach.
- There are 2 swimming pools and 3 tennis courts.
- We cater especially for honeymoon couples.

TA Good morning. It's Mr and Mrs Boswell, isn't it? Did you have a good time in Barbados?

T No, we did not! Where shall we begin? The flight. Why did your brochure say that we (**a**) _____ there in just *two* hours. Concorde takes *four* hours. Didn't you know that?

B Then you said that the hotel (**b**) _____ only twenty minutes from the airport and that it (**c**) _____ large tropical gardens. Not true! The drive from the airport took an hour, and where are the gardens? Your brochure said that these gardens (**d**) _____ directly onto the beach but we couldn't see any tropical gardens, not even one palm tree! The next hotel had them but not ours! And you said there (**e**) _____ swimming pools and tennis courts – not in our hotel!

T And the rooms! You said that we (**f**) _____ wonderful views over the sea, but we couldn't see the sea. Only the weather was good! It was a miserable honeymoon!

3 Reporting words and thoughts

1 **T.73** Report the statements in the next column using the verbs given.

Example
'I'll miss you very much,' he said to her.
He told her that *he'd miss her very much.*

a 'I'm going to Paris soon.'
She said _____ .

b 'The film will be interesting.'
I thought _____ .

c 'I can't help you because I have too much to do.'
She said _____ .

d 'Ann has bought the tickets.'
I was told _____ .

e 'I think it's a stupid idea, and it won't work.'
She said _____ .

f 'Breakfast is served between 7.00 and 9.00.'
The receptionist explained _____ .

g 'I went to Oxford University in the 60s.'
He boasted _____ .

h 'I've never been to America,' she said to me.
She told _____ .

2 **T.74** Report the following questions.

Example
'Where are you going?'
She asked me *where I was going.*

a 'Do you want to go out for a meal?'
She asked me _____ .

b 'Why are you late?' they asked her.
They wondered _____ .

c 'Can I use your phone?'
He asked me_____ .

d 'Where have you come from?'
The customs officer asked me _____ .

e 'How long are you going to be on holiday?'
She wanted to know _____ .

f 'When do you have to go to work?'
She asked me _____ .

g 'Did you post my letter?'
Penny wondered _____ .

h 'Will you be back early?'
He asked her _____ .

3 **T.75** Complete the direct questions.

A is Mrs Smith, who is talking to **B**, a bank manager, about getting a loan.

B Come and sit down, Mrs Smith.

A Thank you very much.

B Now, you want to borrow some money.
(**a**) _____ ?

A Five thousand pounds.

B (**b**) _____ ?

A Because I want to buy a car.

B I see. Could you give me some personal details?
(**c**) _____ ?

A I'm a computer programmer.

B And (**d**) _____ ?

A Twenty thousand pounds a year.

B (**e**) _____ ?

A Yes, I am. I've been married for six years.

B (**f**) _____ ?

A Yes, we've got two children.

B I see you live in a flat. (**g**) _____ ?

A We've lived there for three years.

B Well, that seems fine. I don't think there'll be any problems. (**h**) _____ ?

A I'd like it as soon as possible, actually.

B All right. Let's see what we can do.

4 Report the bank manager's questions.

a First he asked Mrs Smith _____

_____

b Then he wanted to know _____

_____

c He needed to know _____

_____

d She had to tell him _____

_____

e Then he asked _____

_____

f For some reason, he wanted to know _____

_____

g He asked her _____

_____

h Finally he wondered _____

_____

Reported commands

4 *She advised me to ...*

Choose the most appropriate verb from the box to report each of the sentences. Remember they all follow the pattern verb + infinitive.

persuade	order	ask	advise	tell
encourage	invite	beg	remind	

Example
'If I were you, I'd go to the doctor's,' he said to me.
He advised me to go to the doctor's.

a 'Could you possibly do me a favour?' she asked Tom.

_____

b 'Hand in your essays next week,' the teacher told the class.

_____

c 'Don't forget to post the letter,' my wife said to me.

_____

d 'Come and have dinner with us,' Rosie said to John.

_____

e 'You must pay a fine of one hundred pounds,' the judge said to Edward Fox.

_____

f 'Buy the red dress, not the green one,' Betty said to Jane. 'It's much, much nicer.' 'Mmm ... I'm not sure. OK, I'll buy the red one. You're right!' said Jane.

_____

g 'You really should paint professionally,' said Gill to Henry. 'You're really good at it.'

_____

h 'Please, please don't tell my father,' she said to me.

_____

i 'I think you should sell your shares,' his accountant said to Bill.

_____

ask and tell

> 1 Remember that *ask* can be used to report questions and commands, and *tell* can be used to report statements and commands, but the form is different.
>
> **Questions**
> > She **asked** me where I lived.
> > She **asked** me if I wanted a lift.
>
> **Statements**
> > He **told** me he was very unhappy.
> > He **told** his wife that he loved her.
>
> **Commands**
> > He **asked** me to turn the music down.
> > She **told** him to go away.
>
> 2 Notice the negative command.
> > They asked me **not to tell** anyone.
> > She told her son **not to worry**.

5 Statements, questions, and commands

Report the sentences using *ask* or *tell*.

a 'Leave me alone!' she said to him.

_____

b 'Please don't go!' he asked her.

_____

c 'I'm going to bed now,' he said to Anne.

_____

d 'How much do you earn, Dad?' asked Jeremy.

_____

e 'Shut up!' said the teacher to the class.

_____

f 'Can you phone back later, Mr Brown?' asked the secretary.

_____

g 'You did very well in the test,' said the teacher to everyone.

_____

h 'Don't walk on the grass!' the park keeper told the children.

_____

i 'Are you ready to go?' Sally asked Bill.

_____

j 'It's time to get up!' said John to his daughters.

_____

6 Other reporting verbs

Notice the following groups of reporting verbs.

complain admit deny suggest boast	that ...

refuse offer agree promise	to do ...

T.76 Report the sentences, using one of the verbs in the boxes.

Example
'I think it would be a very good idea for you to go to bed,' the doctor said to Paul.
The doctor suggested that Paul went to bed.

a 'Yes, okay. I'll lend you my car but be careful with it!' Peter said to Ann.

_____

b 'Yes, it was me. I stole the money,' said Bill.

_____

c 'But I didn't hit the old lady,' said Bill.

_____

d 'I can speak eleven languages, all perfectly,' said the professor.

_____

e 'I'll leave work early, honest I will,' Angela said.

_____

f 'Ugh! My soup is cold!' said Henry.

_____

g 'I won't help you with your homework. Never!' Jane said to me.

_____

h 'I'll give you a lift to the station, if you like,' Kate said to Megan.

_____

i 'What about if we meet on Thursday?' Mark said to James.
'That's fine,' said James.

_____

speak and *talk*

7 A conversation

⚠️

1 In British English, we use the preposition *to* with the verbs *speak* and *talk*. American English prefers *with*, and this is becoming more common in British English, too.

> *Can I speak **to** you for a minute?*
> *Come and talk **to** me when you're free.*

2 *Talk* suggests that two or more people are having a conversation. It is more common than *speak*.

> *We stayed up all night **talking**.*
> *Can I **talk** to you about my roses? They're all dying.*
> *What do you want to **talk** about?*

3 *Speak* suggests something serious or more formal.

> *I have a complaint. I'd like to **speak** to the manager.*
> *Can you **speak** to your daughter, please, before I hit her. She's behaving awfully.*

Speak also suggests that one person talks more than others.

> *The doctor **spoke** to the audience about the dangers of smoking.*
> *Could you **speak** up, please! We can't hear you at the back.*

4 *Talk* usually suggests the idea of a conversation. *Speak* can refer just to the use of words.

> *I've lost my voice. I can't **speak**.*
> *At the end of the lesson, there was total silence. Nobody **spoke**.*

We use *speak* when talking about languages.

> *How many languages can you **speak**?*

Fill the gaps in the conversation with one of the following verbs in its correct form.

say	tell	explain	speak	talk	reply	ask

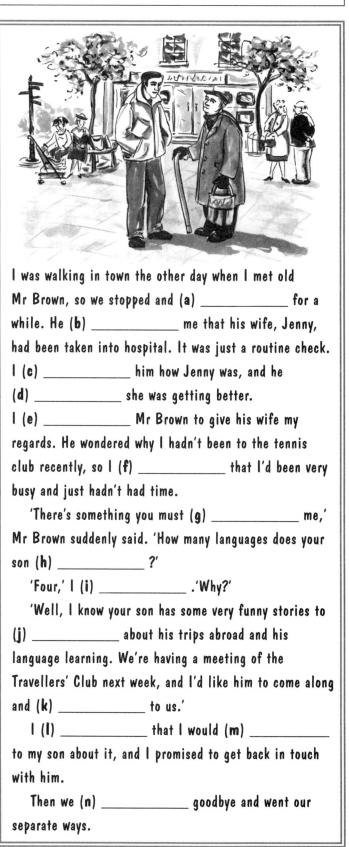

I was walking in town the other day when I met old Mr Brown, so we stopped and **(a)** _____ for a while. He **(b)** _____ me that his wife, Jenny, had been taken into hospital. It was just a routine check. I **(c)** _____ him how Jenny was, and he **(d)** _____ she was getting better.

I **(e)** _____ Mr Brown to give his wife my regards. He wondered why I hadn't been to the tennis club recently, so I **(f)** _____ that I'd been very busy and just hadn't had time.

'There's something you must **(g)** _____ me,' Mr Brown suddenly said. 'How many languages does your son **(h)** _____ ?'

'Four,' I **(i)** _____ .'Why?'

'Well, I know your son has some very funny stories to **(j)** _____ about his trips abroad and his language learning. We're having a meeting of the Travellers' Club next week, and I'd like him to come along and **(k)** _____ to us.'

I **(l)** _____ that I would **(m)** _____ to my son about it, and I promised to get back in touch with him.

Then we **(n)** _____ goodbye and went our separate ways.

Vocabulary

8 Birth, death and marriage

1 Fill the gaps with one of the following words.

> birth   birthday   born

a Where were you _____ ?

b When is your _____ ?

c I was _____ in Africa.

d She gave _____ to a beautiful healthy boy.

e (On an official form) PLACE OF _____

f Congratulations on the _____ of little Albert.

g What are you doing for your _____ this year?

2 Fill the gaps with one of the following words.

> dying   dead   died   death   die

a Shakespeare _____ in 1616.

b Her father's _____ came as a great surprise. He was only 45.

c Those flowers have _____ . Throw them away.

d Every winter thousands of birds _____ in the cold weather.

e 'Is old Bertie Harrison still alive?'

   'I'm sure he's _____ . Didn't he _____ a few years ago?'

f Our poor old cat is _____ . We've had her for fifteen years. She just sits on the chair all day long. She's still got a good appetite, though.

g He was stabbed to _____ by a maniac in a dark alley.

h She screamed when she saw the _____ body lying across the carpet.

i My father _____ three years ago. My mother has been _____ for ages.

j 'When did your dog _____ ? What did it

   _____ of?'
   'He had a heart attack. One minute he was fine, the next minute he was _____ .'

⚠️

1 The verb *marry* is used without a preposition.

   *My sister **married** a plumber.*
   *Will you **marry** me?*

2 *Get married* refers to the change of state between being single and being married.

   *Jo and Andrew are going to **get married** in a registry office.*
   *We **got married** in 1980.*
   *Where did you **get married**?*

   Married refers to the state.

   *Is your brother **married**?*
   *Yes, he's **married** to Ingrid.*

3 *Get married* and *be married* can both be used with the preposition *to*.

   *She got married **to** Gary last weekend.*
   *My sister is married **to** a really nice guy.*

4 *Divorce* is used in a similar way to *marry*.

   *Helen wants to **divorce** Keith.*
   *Jane and Harry **got divorced** last year.*
   *My brother is **divorced**.*

3 Put one of the following words into each gap. Sometimes more than one is possible.

> get married   marry   been married
> got married   married

a 'Are you _____ ?'
   'No, I'm single. But I'd like to

   _____ some day.'

b 'Whatever happened to Ann?'
   'She met a German boy one week and

   _____ him the next.'

c I'm never going to _____ again. Twice is enough.

d How many times have you _____ ?

e Darling, I love you. Will you _____ me?

f We had a lovely wedding. We _____ in a small country church, then had the reception in the local hotel.

g Did you hear? James and Henrietta _____ last week.

h Richard Burton _____ Elizabeth Taylor twice.

i We're engaged, and we're going to _____ next autumn.

Multi-word verbs

9 Multi-word verbs with two particles

Complete the following sentences using one of the combinations in the box.

back on	away from	out of	forward to
on with	down on	up with	

a We've run _____ sugar.
  Could you buy some more?

b We must try to cut _____ the amount
  of money we spend. We're always broke at the
  end of the month.

c Please don't let me disturb you.
  Carry _____ your work.

d Keep _____ me! I've got a terrible cold,
  and I don't want you to catch it.

e She's such a snob. She looks _____ anyone
  that doesn't have all the things she has.

f Children grow _____ their clothes so
  quickly. It costs a fortune!

g How do you get _____ your parents? OK?

h I don't know how you put _____ such
  noisy neighbours. It would drive me crazy.

i When I look _____ my childhood, I realize
  how unhappy I was.

j I'm really looking _____ our holidays next
  week. I'm so excited!

Pronunciation

10 Word stress

T.77   All these words appear in Unit 12 of the
Student's book. Mark the stressed syllable.

Examples
honeymoon   promotion   Madrid

a funeral   g divorced   m impatient
b invite   h sympathy   n confident
c invitation   i engaged   o contradict
d offer   j godmother   p forever
e argue   k congratulate
f argument   l celebration

11 *had* or *would*?

'd is the contracted form of both *had* and *would*.

Example
I'd like to come. = *would*
He asked if I'd been to America. = *had*

T.78   Transcribe the following sentences.
They all contain *'d*.
Write *had* or *would* in the brackets after each one.

Example
/wid lʌv tə miːt jɔː mʌðə/
We'd love to meet your mother. (would)

a /ʃi sed ðət ʃiːd siːn hɪm/

   _____

   (   )

b /ʃi sed ðət ʃiːd siː hɪm suːn/

   _____

   (   )

c /ðeɪ ɑːskt ɪf wiːd gɪv ðəm ə lɪft/

   _____

   (   )

d /ðeɪ ɑːskt ɪf wiːd gɪvn hə ðə bʊk/

   _____

   (   )

e /hi təʊld hə hiːd lʌvd hər ə lɒŋ taɪm/

   _____

   (   )

f /hi təʊld hə hiːd lʌv hə fərevə/

   _____

   (   )

g /wi ɑːskt wen ðeɪd met iːtʃ ʌðə/

   _____

   (   )

h /wi ɑːskt wen ðeɪd miːt iːtʃ ʌðər əgen/

   _____

   (   )

Key

Unit 1

Auxiliary verbs

1 The forms of *do*, *be*, and *have*

b I don't work in a bank.
c Do you work in an office?
d My father works in an office.
e My mother doesn't work in an office.
f Does your father work in an office?

b I'm not learning Portuguese.
c Are you learning Spanish?
d My father's learning Spanish.
e My mother isn't learning Spanish.
f Is your father learning Spanish?

b I didn't see the River Ganges.
c Did you see the Taj Mahal?
d My father saw the Taj Mahal.
e My mother didn't see the Taj Mahal.
f Did your father see the Taj Mahal?

b I haven't met Prince Charles.
c Have you met the Queen?
d My father's met the Queen.
e My mother hasn't met the Queen.
f Has your father met the Queen?

2 Full verb or auxiliary verb?

a	A	e	A	i	A
b	F	f	F	j	A
c	F	g	F	k	A
d	A	h	F	l	F

3 Contracted forms

a She's got two brothers and she doesn't get on with either of them.

b He has no brothers or sisters, he's an only child.

c We weren't interested in the film so we didn't stay until the end.

d He didn't go to the party because he had a cold.

e They're getting married when they've saved enough money.

f John's not/isn't sure where Jill is.

g She's feeding the dog. It's always fed at six o'clock.

h I don't want them to know who I am.

i Don't you understand what I'm saying?

j Where's the man who's been to New Zealand?

4 *My computer's gone wrong!*

Exercise 1

a	've got	g	don't
b	isn't/'s not	h	did
c	's	i	didn't
d	don't	j	have
e	'm	k	haven't
f	was	l	does

Exercise 2

a Why is Val ringing the Apple Helpline?
Because she's got a terrible problem with her computer.

b Which company does Val work for?
She doesn't work for a company, she's self-employed.

c What was she doing when her computer stopped?
She was working away happily.

d Why can't Val remember the message?
Because she didn't understand it.

e Has she switched her computer off?
No, she hasn't.

5 Making questions

Exercise 1

a What are you wearing at the moment?

b Where were you living when you started school?

c Where did you go on holiday when you were a child?

d Do you play any sports at the weekend?

e What time did you get up this morning?

f Have you ever been to Egypt to see the pyramids?

g Do you look like your mother?

Exercise 2

a What languages does he speak?
b What did you have?
c How much did they pay?
d How many kittens did she have?
e What film's she going to see?
f Who's she writing to?
g What do you do?
h Where did you go?

6 Negatives and short answers

Exercise 1

a	hasn't	e	have
b	am	f	do
c	don't	g	did
d	didn't	h	isn't

Exercise 2 (Sample answers)

a Yes, I am. I'm going skiing.
b Yes, I did. We went to Barbados.
c No, I haven't, but I'd like to go.
d Yes, I do. I travel in my job.
e No, she doesn't.

have/have got

7 Sentence completion

a didn't have
b Have you got/Do you have
c 's got/has
d 'll have
e haven't got/don't have
f has had
g are having
h have
i Did you have
j 've got/have
k does she usually have

Vocabulary

8 Holidays and medicine

Exercise 1

Things to take	Activities
rucksack	water-skiing
traveller's cheques	exploring
swimming costume	sunbathing
beach towel	relaxing
suntan lotion	sight-seeing

People	Places to stay
ski instructor	caravan
travel agent	farmhouse
flight attendant	guest-house
tour guide	youth hostel
	camp-site

Exercise 2

Things that doctors give you	Illnesses/problems
X-ray	sore throat
injection	constipation
prescription	diarrhoea
operation	rash
check-up	sprain
pills	cough

People	Parts of the body
surgeon	heart
patient	kidney
specialist	stomach
	lungs
	liver

Pronunciation

9 Phonetic script
Exercise 1

a breakfast   g musical instrument
b computer   h tradition
c knowledge   i journalist
d hungry   j weapons
e earth   k statue
f newspaper

Exercise 2

a the grass is green
b the wind is never seen
c the birds to build a nest
d the trees to take a rest
e the moon is not quite round
f the missing bit be found
g lights the stars
h makes the lightning
i the rainbow in the sky
j the fluffy clouds so high

Prepositions

10 Verb + preposition

a with   f about
b in   g about
c on   h of
d to   i for
e to   j about

Grammar words

11 Terminology

a full verb
b pronoun
c countable noun
d modal auxiliary verb
e adverb
f adjective
g comparative adjective
h infinitive with *to*
i indefinite article
j preposition
k *-ing* form of the verb
l definite article
m superlative adjective
n past participle
o uncountable noun

Unit 2

Present Simple

1 Profiles

Ursula Buhlmann: b, e, g
Vichai: a, c, f
Sue Morris and Geoff: h, d, i

2 Sentence completion

a run
b is called
c closes
d don't go
e has got/has
f takes … to walk
g starts
h doesn't provide
i graduate   want
j have
k earn
l hate

3 Questions

a What does the milkbar sell?/… do milkbars …
b What time does it open?
c Why don't Sue and Geoff go to the movies any more?
d What does Ursula's father do?
e Where does Ursula live?
f How many pupils are in each class at Ursula's school?
g How many lessons does Ursula have?
h How long is her lunch-break?
i What does Ursula want to do when she leaves school?
j Who does Vichai live with?
k What does he usually have for breakfast?
l What does he enjoy playing?
m Does he like living in Bangkok?

4 Negatives

(Sample answers)
a Vegetarians don't eat meat.
b A vegan doesn't eat any animal products.
c An atheist doesn't believe in God.
d I'm unemployed. I haven't got a job.
e My father's bald. He hasn't got any hair.
f They are penniless. They don't have any money.
g Selfish people don't think of other people.

Pronunciation

5 -s at the end of a word

/ɪz/
closes messages sandwiches places

/s/
shops hates cooks cheques products graduates minutes wants

/z/
girls hours kids boys earns keys loves lessons schools things lives

Present states and actions

6 Present Simple and Present Continuous

Exercise 2 (Sample answers)
Rita is a traffic warden. She works in the city centre, and checks parked cars. She wears a uniform and gives parking tickets.
At the moment she isn't working, she's in her kitchen. She's wearing a dress and an apron. Her children are in the kitchen, too. One of them is sitting at the table, and the other is in a baby chair.

Gerald is a football coach. Every weekday he spends all morning on the training pitch, working with players. They train hard, and practise moves.
At the moment Gerald isn't working, he's on holiday in the Caribbean. He's having a drink on the beach. He's wearing a swimming costume and sunglasses.

Tony and **Peggy** are organic farmers. They get up very early and work in the fields most days. They grow vegetables and wheat, and raise hens on their farm.
It's evening and Tony and Peggy aren't working, they're in the pub with some friends. Tony's drinking beer, and Peggy's drinking wine. They're laughing and chatting with their friends.

7 Present Simple or Present Continuous?

Exercise 1

a [✗] I think you are very impolite.
b [✔]
c [✗] Why are you leaving so early? Aren't you enjoying the party?
d [✗] Nobody ever laughs at my husband's jokes. It's so embarrassing.
e [✔]
f [✔]
g [✗] I don't see what your problem is.
h [✔]
i [✗] He never knows the answer.

Exercise 2

Conversation 1

a are you doing   e are you going
b am packing   f don't know
c am leaving   g know
d don't understand   h is meeting

Conversation 2

a is that man doing
b is waiting
c don't open
d Do you think
e is taking
f is walking

Exercise 3

a I'm thinking of learning how to fly a plane.
  I think that's a good idea.
b Do you see what I mean?
  What time are you seeing the bank manager?
c She has a wonderful suntan.
  She's having a wonderful time in Spain.

8 *always*

a You're always doing that.
b We always go there on holiday.
c They're always going on holiday.
d You're always buying new clothes.
e I always go by bus.
f … it's always breaking down.

Present passive

9 Past participles

a spoken   f taken
b produced   g employed
c included   h grown
d decorated   i pulled down
e made   j delivered

10 Active or passive?

a arrive   h is searched
b are checked i wait
c keep   j is called
d are taken   k are told
e is checked   l board
f are x-rayed m are shown
g are given

11 A poem

Exercise 2

Passive: is made (×3) Is … being born

Active: make (×2) keeps eat wonder dream takes strikes sets 's dying

Vocabulary

12 Synonyms and antonyms

Adjective	Opposite (Adj + prefix)	Opposite (different word)
polite	impolite	rude
expensive	inexpensive	cheap
interesting	uninteresting	boring
correct	incorrect	wrong
attractive	unattractive	ugly

Adjective	Opposite (Adj + prefix)	Opposite (different word)
fashionable	unfashionable	out of date
intelligent	unintelligent	stupid
usual	unusual	strange/rare
kind	unkind	cruel
formal	informal	casual
modest	immodest	arrogant

Multi-word verbs

13 *look* and *be*

Exercise 1

a look it up
b looking for
c Look out
d am looking forward/look forward
e Look at
f looked after

Exercise 2

a in   f up
b away   g in on
c on   h off
d off   i off
e up to   j up

Unit 3

Past Simple and Past Continuous

1 A sad story

Exercise 1

2 ran up   4 was waiting
8 killed   1 was watering the plants
5 arrived   8 were leaving
6 put up   1 was playing
2 called   7 were having tea
3 rang
6 rescued
8 ran him over
2 couldn't get down
7 invited them for tea
4 tried to tempt him down

Exercise 2

a was watering the plants
b was playing
c ran up
d called
e couldn't get down
f rang
g was waiting
h tried to tempt him down
i arrived
j put up
k rescued
l invited them for tea
m were having tea
n were leaving
o ran him over
p killed

2 Correcting facts

a Mrs Taylor wasn't cutting the grass, she was watering the plants.
b Billy wasn't sleeping in the garden, he was playing.
c Billy didn't jump over the wall, he ran up a tree.
d Mrs Taylor didn't ring the Police, she rang the Fire Brigade.
e The Fire Brigade didn't use a rope, they used their ladder.
f He didn't die when he fell from the tree, he died when they ran him over.

3 Past Simple or Past Continuous?

a was working   opened   rushed
b stood   walked   closed
c walked   was wearing
d Didn't you meet   were working
e saw   were sitting
f walked   handed
g was listening   was doing
h didn't they visit   were staying
i was passing   knocked
  (*As he passed* is also possible.)
j were you writing   crashed

4 A holiday in Madeira

a decided   j couldn't
b left   k was staying
c was raining   l went
d landed   m saw
e was shining   n was getting
f was blowing   o returned
g took   p spent
h was signing   q felt
i tapped   r ended

5 *What did he do?*
What was he doing?

a Jack was driving home from work when he saw the accident.
b When he saw the accident, he pulled the young man out of the van and took him straight to hospital.
c John was repairing his car when he heard the good news.
d He gave his wife a big kiss and took the family out for a slap-up meal.
e People were standing in queues and chatting when the robbers burst in.
f Martin Webb suffered a heart attack.

Past Perfect

6 Regular and irregular verbs

Infinitive	Past Simple	Past participle
grow	grew	grown
leave	left	left
fall	fell	fallen

Infinitive	Past Simple	Past participle
find	found	found
sell	sold	sold
feel	felt	felt
drive	drove	driven
fly	flew	flown
leave	left	left
travel	travelled	travelled
lie	lied	lied
win	won	won
spend	spent	spent

7 Choosing the right tense

a sat
b had been
c had lived
d was
e hadn't managed
f had taken
g had been
h went
i got
j felt
k was
l had been
m decided

8 Sentence completion

a … because she had overslept and missed the bus.
b She had sent him to a good school, but he hadn't done any work and had failed his exams.
c He had stolen money from his employer and had spent it on drugs.
d I had never flown before.
e He had been in the same job for ten years.
f I was sure I had seen him somewhere before.
g … but he hadn't always been poor. He had been a millionaire, but his business had collapsed and he had lost everything.
h I hadn't had anything to eat all day.

9 *had* or *would*?

a would
b would
c had
d had
e would
f had

Past Simple active and passive

10 Biographies

Helen Keller

a were caused
b didn't know
c found
d were told
e came
f taught
g had
h was offered
i toured
j was made

Charles Blondin

a was born
b was taught
c became
d was put
e walked
f watched
g were carried
h fell
i wasn't killed
j died

Amy Johnson

a joined
b was taught
c was introduced
d held
e tried
f didn't succeed
g returned
h were married
i was written
j disappeared

11 *Somebody did that!*

a The bank was robbed last night.
b I was told to wait outside.
c She wasn't invited to the party.
d They were driven to the airport.
e We weren't sent any tickets.
f Was the missing child found?
h Were you disturbed (by anything) in the night?

while, during and *for*

12 Gap filling

a during
b while
c for
d While
e for
f During
g for
h while
i during
j during
k for
l while
m during (= while we were eating, not for the meal)

Vocabulary

13 Adverbs

a I got up late this morning, but *fortunately* I *just* managed to catch the bus.
b 'Hi, Pete. How are you?'
   'My name's John, *actually*, but don't worry.'/ '*Actually*, my name's …'
c In the middle of the picnic it *suddenly* began to rain./*Suddenly*, in the …
d I *only* saw Mary at the party. I didn't see anyone else.
e I *only* gave a present to John, not to anyone else.
f Jane and I have *always* been friends. We went to school *together*. We were *even* born in the same hospital.
g 'You know I applied for that job.'
   'Which job?'
   'The one based in Paris.'
   'No. I don't know anything about it.'
   '*Anyway*, I didn't get it.'
h 'I didn't like it.'
   'I didn't like it, *either*.'
i 'I like it.'
   'I like it, *too*.'
j Everybody in our family *really* loves ice-cream, *especially* me.
k The traffic to the airport was *so* bad that we *nearly* missed the plane.
l I'm tall *enough* to be a policeman, but I haven't got *enough* qualifications.

Prepositions

14 *in, at, on* for time

a 'It's my birthday next week.'
   'When?'
   '*On* Monday.'
   'What time were you born?'
   '*At* 8.00 *in* the morning.'

b 'I'm meeting Alan this evening.'
   'What time?'
   '*At* six.'

c 'What did you do *at* the weekend?'
   '*On* Friday evening we went to a party. We slept in late *on* Saturday morning, and then *in* the afternoon we went shopping. *At* 7.00 some friends came round for a drink. We didn't do anything *on* Sunday. What about you?'

d The weather in England is unreliable. *In* summer it can be hot, but it often rains *in* April and June. Last year the summer was awful. The best English weather is *in* spring and autumn.

e I learned to drive *in* 1980 *at* the age of 17. My brother learned *at* the same time as me, but I passed first.

f I'll phone you next week. *On* Thursday, maybe. *In* the afternoon. *At* about 3.00. OK?

g I don't see my parents much. *At* Christmas, usually, and *in* the holidays.

Pronunciation

15 Words that sound the same

a She threw the ring through the window and into the garden.
b The soldiers wore khaki uniforms when they went to war.
c I must warn you that ties must be worn at the Ritz.
d The police caught the burglar and he ended up in court in front of Judge Jordan.
e I blew up six red balloons and ten blue ones for the party.
f We knew that Sue and Jim had bought a new car.
g I saw Jack at the doctor's with a sore throat.
h The book I read had a red cover.
i We rode our horses along the narrow road.

Unit 4

have to/don't have to

1 What do they have to do?

Exercise 1

c 'I have to wear smart suits.'

b 'I always have to be home before midnight.'

c 'I often have to travel overseas.'

b 'My dad usually has to work in the evenings.'

a 'I don't have to get up at 6.30 am any more.'

c 'My husband has to take our children to school every morning.'

a 'My wife has to go to hospital every week.'

b 'I have to get good results in my exams.'

b 'My sister doesn't have to help with the housework.'

Exercise 2

a Why do you often have to travel overseas?

b Why do you always have to be home before midnight?

c Why don't you have to get up at 6.30 am any more?

d Why does your dad usually have to work in the evenings?

e Why does your wife have to go to hospital every week?

f Why doesn't your sister have to help with the housework?

g Why does your husband have to take your children to school every morning?

h Why do you have to get good results in your exams?

2 Forms of have to

a has to   doesn't have to

b had to   didn't have to

c will have to

d having to

e Do we/Will we have to

f Did your grandmother have to

g don't have to

h will I have to

can and allowed to

3 Who says?

Exercise 1

a A traffic warden. In the street.

b A waiter/maitre d'. At a restaurant.

c A customs official. At customs.

d A librarian. In a library.

e A flight attendant. On a plane.

f A prisoner. In prison.

Exercise 2 (Sample answers)

a You can't make a noise. You can visit the patients.

b You can't touch the exhibits. You can look at objects.

c You aren't allowed to dive in the shallow end. You can dive in the diving area.

d You aren't allowed to pick the flowers. You can sit on the benches.

4 Dialogues for permission

n Jill	j Sam
i Jack	b Anna
a Jill	e Sam
c Jack	d Anna
g Jill	k Sam
l Jack	m Anna
f Jill	h Sam

5 can and be able to

Exercise 1

a can't

b Can/Could

c to be able to

d couldn't

e couldn't

f to be able to

g will be able to

h could   couldn't

i can't/won't be able to

j Being able to

Exercise 2

a managed to

b couldn't

c could

d Could

e couldn't

f Did you manage to

g managed to

h could

i could

must, should and have to

6 must or have to?

a must

b have to

c must

d have to

e must

f have to

g must

h have to

7 Giving advice

(Sample answers)

a You should get rid of the television!

b You should buy another one.

c You should try to cut down on coffee.

d He should start a new hobby.

e You should have a haircut!

8 mustn't or don't have to?

a mustn't

b don't have to

c mustn't

d doesn't have to

e don't have to

f don't have to

g mustn't

h mustn't

i don't have to

Vocabulary and pronunciation

9 Nationality words

Exercise 1

Country	Adjective
'Italy	I'talian
'Germany	'German
Greece	Greek
'England	'English
'Finland	'Finnish
the 'Netherlands	Dutch
'China	Chi'nese
'Scotland	'Scottish

Exercise 2

The Italians eat a lot of pasta.

The Greeks had many great philosophers.

The Germans are good at business.

The Dutch grow lots of tulips.

The English talk a lot about the weather.

The Chinese cook lots of noodles.

The Finns like taking saunas.

The Scots wear kilts.

Exercise 3 (Sample answers)

'Ireland   'Irish

The Irish enjoy talking.

Spain   'Spanish

The Spanish eat a lot of fish.

Ja'pan   Japa'nese

The Japanese don't have many holidays.

'Russia   'Russian

The Russians wear fur hats.

'Sweden   'Swedish

The Swedes go cross-country skiing.

'Switzerland   Swiss

The Swiss make good cheese.

'Mexico   'Mexican

The Mexicans like hot food.

Au'stralia   Au'stralian

The Australians love cricket.

'Turkey   'Turkish

The Turks drink very strong coffee.

Pronunciation

10 Correcting wrong information

Mr H Good morning Miss Maddox.

Mrs M It's Mrs Maddox actually.

Mr H Oh yes. Mrs Mary Maddox of ...

Mrs M Mrs Maureen Maddox.

Mr H Yes, of course. Maureen Maddox of twenty-three ...

Mrs M Twenty-two, actually.

Mr H Twenty-two Hillside Lane, Chesterfield.

Mrs M Hillside Road, Chesterfield.

Mr H Ah yes. Now Mrs Maddox, I believe you want to borrow five hundred pounds.

Mrs M No, in fact, I want to borrow five thousand pounds. Haven't you got my letter?

Mr H No, I'm afraid not. But I understand you want to open a music shop for your son.

Mrs M Oh, dear me, no. I want to open a gift shop for my daughter. Don't you think you should read my letter, Mr Hardcastle?

Mr H A gift shop for your daughter. Well, I'll send you a form to …

Mrs M But you sent me a form last week, and I'm ringing because I have some queries about it.

Mr H Oh, so you've filled in the form …

Mrs M No, I haven't filled in the form. I can't fill it in because I don't understand it. That's why I'm ringing.

Mr H Oh I see! You want to ask me some questions about the form.

Mrs M Not any more. I don't want to ask you questions about anything!! Good bye!

Multi-word verbs

11 Separable or inseparable?

Exercise 2
a Turn it down!
b … but you must look after it.
c Don't throw it away.
d Look at it!
e I'm really looking forward to it.
f … or did you make it up?
g I tried it on but it was too small.
h Pick it up!
i Give it back to me!
j Work it out for yourself!

Unit 5
Future forms (1)

1 *will* or *going to*?
a 'll get
b 'll give you
c are going to have   'll get
d will you be   'll
e will   will/is going to
f 'll give it
g are you going to   'll pay

h are you going to   'll do some
i will it   will it be
j 'll love it   are you going to

2 *Where are they going?*
a Where's she going?
  She's going shopping.
b Where are they going?
  They're going skating.
c Where's she going?
  She's going fishing.
d Where are they going?
  They're going skiing.
e Where's she going?
  She's going sailing.

3 *I'm sure they'll …*
a 'll feel better
b he'll help
c won't give me any
d it'll rain
e 'll need glasses
f 'll get sunburnt
g won't like it
h won't pass/'ll fail

4 Making offers
(Sample answers)
a I'll get you one.
b I'll see who it is.
c I'll lend you some.
d I'll give you a lift.
e I'll carry one.

Future forms (2)

5 Making arrangements
Exercise 1
a am having   f is delivering
b are you inviting g is … making
c are coming   h are you giving
d are staying   i am booking
e are you getting   j are travelling

Exercise 2
c does not sound very natural with *going to*; we do not usually use *going to* with the verbs *go* and *come*.

6 Choosing the correct form
a ✔ 'Yes, we have. We're going to Italy.'
  ✘ 'Yes, we have. We'll go to Italy.'
b ✘ 'Oooh! It's agony! But I see the dentist this afternoon.'
  ✔ 'Oooh! It's agony! But I'm seeing the dentist this afternoon.'
c ✘ 'Ah, but the weather forecast says it's raining.'
  ✔ 'Ah, but the weather forecast says it's going to rain.'

d ✔ 'Yes, that's right. It's being delivered tomorrow.'
  ✘ 'Yes, that's right. It will be delivered tomorrow.'
e ✔ 'Don't worry. We won't tell anybody.'
  ✘ 'Don't worry. We're not telling anybody.'
f ✘ 'It's OK. I'm going to lend you some.'
  ✔ 'It's OK. I'll lend you some.'
g ✘ 'We've just learnt that we'll have twins!'
  ✔ 'We've just learnt that we're going to have twins!'
h ✔ 'I'd love to, but John's taking me out tonight.'
  ✘ 'I'd love to, but John'll take me out tonight.'

somebody, nobody, anybody, everybody

7 Compound words
a anyone/anybody
b something
c anyone/anybody   nobody/no one
d anyone/anybody
e somewhere
f anything
g somewhere
h nothing
i anywhere
j everybody/everyone
k Anything
l Nobody/No one   nothing
m Everyone/Everybody
n Somewhere/Anywhere

Vocabulary

8 *make* or *do*?
Exercise 1

make

up my mind	a profit
a mess	a noise
a complaint	a phone call
sure that	friends with
my bed	a will
money	love
a speech	progress

do

the shopping	my best
someone a favour	business with
the housework	exercises
nothing	the washing-up

Exercise 2

a make a phone call
b made up her mind
c do nothing
d make a noise
e doing my best
f made a complaint
g making any progress
h do me a favour
i making a will
j made friends
k do exercises
l make sure
m Make love

Prepositions

9 *in, at, on* for place

a I met my husband *in* Italy. He was *in* a shop, buying pasta. I was *in* a queue, waiting to buy some bread.

b Last night I was *in* the kitchen when I lost my glasses. I looked *on* all the shelves and *in* all the cupboards. I thought I'd put them *in* one of the drawers, but they weren't there. They certainly weren't *on* the table or *on* the floor. Had I left them *at* work? Were they *in* the car? Then I realized where they were. They were *on* my nose.

c 'Where were you at 2.00?' '*On* the beach.' '*At* work.' '*In* Manchester.' '*At* Sally's house doing my homework.' '*In* the bath.' '*At* home.' '*On* a boat.'

Pronunciation

10 Vowel sounds and spelling

Exercise 1

a weather /e/   d women /ɪ/
b sugar /ʊ/   e uncle /ʌ/
c woman /ʊ/   f half /ɑː/

Exercise 2

a break   e breath
b won't   f wooden
c wonder   g work
d hungry   h ferry

Exercise 3

a petrol   f statue
b yoghurt   g freezing
c interesting   h luxury
d thought   i daughter
e breakfast   j smooth

Unit 6

like

1 Questions with *like*

Exercise 1

(Sample answers)

a I like working in small groups most.
b I like working with a partner.
c I'd like to have less homework.
d It's very nice; it's not very big, but there's a nice blue notice-board, and some green plants. It's light and comfortable.
e They're fantastic!
f It's not very good, but it's getting better.
g I'd like to speak more in class, and write more at home.

Exercise 2

a What's your job like?
b Who do you look like?
c What did you look like when you were a child?
d Would you like coffee or tea?
e Do you like tennis?
f Would you like to come to the cinema this evening?
g What's your new teacher like?
h How are your parents?

Exercise 3

a What was it like?
b What was that like?
c what were they like?
d What do they look like?
e What was that like?
f did you like
g would you like

2 *like* versus *would like*

Exercise 1

a A I only like white chocolate.
   B I don't. I can't stand it.
b A Would you like a lift?
   B It's OK. I'll get the bus.
c A Would you like some more cake?
   B I'd love some. It's delicious.
d A Would you like a cold drink?
   B I'd love one. I'm very thirsty.
e A Don't you like your boss?
   B I hate him.
f A I don't like cabbage.
   B Really? I love it.
g A I wouldn't like to work for her!
   B Nor would I.
h A Would you like to come to dinner?
   B I'd love to. That's very kind.
i A What do you like doing at the weekends?
   B Nothing.

Exercise 2

a ✘ What do you like to do tonight?
  ✔ What would you like to do tonight?
b ✔ Where do you like going on holiday?
  ✘ Where would you like to go on holiday?
c ✘ Do you like Coke?
  ✔ Would you like a Coke?
d ✔ What sort of books do you like reading?
  ✘ What sort of books would you like to read?
e ✔ Do you like your teacher?
  ✘ Would you like to be a teacher?
f ✘ Do you like your teacher?
  ✔ Would you like to be a teacher?

3 *like* versus *as*

a as … as   f like   k as
b like   g like   l like
c as   h as   m like
d like   i like   n as
e like   j like   o like

Verb patterns

4 Choosing the correct form

a you to be   e to seeing
b smoking   f do
c to work   g to go
d to tell you h watching

5 A puzzle

6 Using a dictionary

Right: a, c, d, e, i, j

Correct versions

b Would you like to come round to our house for a meal some time?

f I always like to pay my bills on time.

g He thinks we should go, and I agree.

h She thinks she's right, but I don't agree.

k She thought we should go, and I agreed.

l They agreed to discuss the problem further.

Relative clauses

7 Subject or object?

a Where are the scissors ~~that~~ I bought yesterday?

b I want you to meet the woman who taught me how to drive. ✔

c The meal ~~that~~ you cooked was delicious.

d I like animals that don't make a mess. ✔

e The film ~~that~~ I've always wanted to see is on TV tonight.

f The flat ~~that~~ they bought was very expensive.

g The room in our house that is most used is the kitchen. ✔

h I didn't like the meal ~~that~~ we had yesterday.

i The people who work here are very interesting. ✔

j The man ~~who~~ you were talking about has just come in the room.

8 Gap filling

a I received a letter this morning *which/that* really upset me.

b Toby, a boy I went to school with, is ill in hospital.

c He's going to have an operation *which/that* could save his life.

d Toby, *whose* parents both died a few years ago, is the same age as me.

e I recently went back to the town *where* I was born.

f The people *who* used to live next door moved a long time ago.

g I met a girl I used to go out with.

h She told me a story I found hard to believe.

i She said she'd married a man *who* had been married ten times before.

j Apparently, he lost all his money gambling, *which* really annoyed her.

Vocabulary

9 Antonyms and synonyms

Exercise 1

a a married person
   a return ticket

b a weak man
   light beer

c a poor person
   plain food

d a sour apple
   dry wine

e a mild curry
   a cold drink

f fair hair
   a light room

Exercise 2

a a wealthy/well-off woman

b an amusing story

c a smart person

d a messy room

e a naughty child

f correct information

g kind/nice/helpful people

h a stupid/foolish person

i an intelligent person

j a great/brilliant/fantastic/an excellent idea

k dreadful/terrible news

l revolting/horrible food

Multi-word verbs

10 Multi-word verbs + objects

Exercise 1

sort out	a problem
put out	a fire
fill in	a form
find out	information
try on	clothes in a shop
try out	a new idea, a new drug
bring up	children
clear up	a mess
take back	something you don't want to a shop
put off	a meeting to another time
put away	clothes in a cupboard

Exercise 2

a put them away

b find out

c Take them back

d sort it all out

e put it out

f try out

g try these jeans on

h put it off

i clear everything up

j Fill it in

Pronunciation

11 Sentence stress

a Jack's very short.

b Do you want a single ticket?

c Does Liz like red wine?

d Did Paul say the film was boring?

e Do Jane and Paul like going for walks?

f Would you like a hot drink?

g I really liked school when I was young.

h Have you got a headache?

Unit 7

Present Perfect

1 *How many did she …?*
How many has she …?

Exercise 1

a has she written	e did he make
b did she write	f has he made
c has she made	g has he painted
d did she make	h did he paint

Exercise 2

c Sonja Samms has recently married her co-star, Richard Ledmann.

g David Hockney has lived in Los Angeles for many years because he prefers the light there.

a Sylvia Conran has just published a biography of Charles Dickens.

f Andy Cushing has played with three different bands over the years.

d Marilyn Monroe committed suicide in 1962.

e Bob Marley's band was called *The Wailers*.

b Jane Austen never married.

h Van Gogh only sold one painting while he was alive.

Exercise 3

a did they	c did it take
b did he move	d was he when he

Exercise 4

The Present Perfect and the Past Simple.

2 Choosing the correct tense

a was born	f was painted
b has been	g has also designed
c studied	h has lived
d has travelled	i has never married
e went	j lives

3 Dialogues

a A You're brown! Where have you been?
   B We've been on holiday.
   A Where did you go?
   B We went to Spain.
   A When did you get back?
   B Last night. The plane landed at 6.00 in the evening.

b A What have you done to your finger?
   B I've cut myself./I cut …
   A How did you do that?
   B I was cooking and the knife slipped.
   A Have you put anything on it?
   B No. It's not that bad.

4 *been* or *gone*?

a gone   e been
b been   f been
c been   g gone
d gone

5 Time expressions

Exercise 1

	Past Simple	Present Perfect
in	✔	✗
ago	✔	✗
at	✔	✗
just	✔	✔
before	✔	✔
yet	✗	✔
already	✗	✔
never	✔	✔

Exercise 2

a I've *just* heard you're getting married.
b Have you read the newspaper *yet*?
c I've *already* done my homework.
d Have you *ever* been to Thailand?
e I haven't seen the film *yet*.

Exercise 3

a Excuse me! I haven't finished yet.
b No, thanks. I've just put one out.
c He's just gone out.
d I've already fed her.
e Has the match finished yet?

6 Talking about you

(Sample answers)

a Yes, I have. I went yesterday.
b I bought some food and some videos.
c I haven't spent anything today yet.
d I've had a very busy day!
e Yes, I have. I saw a very good film two weeks ago.
f I haven't had any lessons yet.

7 Correcting mistakes

a How long have you known the teacher?
b This is the first time I have eaten honey with spaghetti.
c What did you do last night?
d I have studied English for four years.
e When did you get your hair cut?
f I saw Peter yesterday.

Tense review

8 Curriculum vitae

Exercise 2

I do you live
I Have you been
H went
I did you study
H English   Sociology
I Do you speak
H speak French
I Have you ever lived
H have   lived   worked
I did you do
H worked as a porter in a children's hospital
I are you doing
H am working with disabled children in Botton Village,
I have you been working
H April 1996

Exercise 3

a was born
b lives
c studied
d learned   was living/lived
e has been working/has worked
f enjoys (going)
g used

Present Perfect passive

9 Active or passive?

a 's just been promoted
b 've applied
c have you been made
d has just lost
e has taken
f has been given
g has risen
h has been called
i haven't been offered
j have you saved

10 Two newspaper stories

Exercise 1

The Loch Ness wallet

a dropped   d has been found
b were lost   e was discovered
c rang   f have been put

Picassos taken in £40 raid

a have just announced
b have been stolen
c have been valued
d were taken
e did not go off
f was not discovered
g have so far been found

Exercise 2

a When did Gaspar Sanchez lose his wallet?
b When was it found?
c What has been stolen from Stockholm's Modern Museum?
d Have the paintings been valued?
e When were they stolen?
f Have any clues been found?

Vocabulary

11 Words with more than one meaning

Exercise 2

Look in your dictionary for answers to this exercise.

Pronunciation

12 Phonetic script and word stress

Exercise 1

Two syllables

a business   f career
b forget   g resign
c apply   h retired
d foreign   i factory
e kidnapped   j degree

Three syllables

k employer   p director
l employee   q uniform
m interview   r murderer
n millionaire   s redundant
o politics   t magazine

Four syllables

u unemployment x application
v interviewee   y resignation
w politician   z interpreter

Exercise 2

Stress pattern	Words
●•	a, d, e, i
•●	b, c, f, g, h, j
•●•	k, p, s
●••	m, o, q, r
••●	l, n, t
••●•	u, w, x, y
•••●	v
•●••	z

Prepositions

13 Noun + preposition

a	on	g	with
b	out of	h	for
c	for	i	on
d	on	j	in
e	between	k	of
f	about	l	to

Unit 8

Conditionals (1) and time clauses

1 Matching

a If we can afford it, we'll buy a new car soon. The one we have now is very unreliable.

c If I don't hear from you tomorrow, I'll expect a call the next day. I need to speak to you again soon.

d If the pain gets too bad, take another dose of painkillers. That should help.

e If the bus doesn't come soon, I'll be late for school. That'll be the second time this week.

f If you can't see what you want in the window, step inside. There are lots more things to see in the shop.

g If I'm going to be late, I'll let you know. You can put my supper in the oven.

h If Peter rings, tell him I never want to see him again. And don't tell him where I've gone!

2 Dialogues

Shopping		Menu	
a	Tom	b	Tom
g	Fran	h	Fran
l	Tom	n	Tom
c	Fran	d	Fran
e	Tom	k	Tom
m	Fran	f	Fran
i	Tom	p	Tom
j	Fran		
o	Tom		

3 Useful tips

(Sample answers)

a If you have a nosebleed, drop a key down the back of your neck.

b If you spill red wine on a carpet, sprinkle salt on it immediately.

c If you get dandruff, try using a special shampoo.

d If you have a hangover, drink lots of fizzy water.

e If you can't get to sleep, count sheep!

f If you can't stop biting your nails, wear gloves!

4 Combining sentences

a I want to speak to you before you go out.

b I'm going to read a lot of books while we're away on holiday.

c I'll get in touch as soon as I get back.

d Would you like a cup of tea before you go to work?

e I'll tell you all our news when I see you.

f I won't speak to her until she says sorry.

g Let's phone Jack now before it's too late.

h Don't go without me. Wait until I'm ready.

i I'll give you a ring after we get back from holiday.

j Can you feed the cats while we're away on holiday?

Conditionals (2) and would

5 Sentence completion

a If we had enough money, we'd have a holiday.

b If I knew the answer, I'd tell you.

c I'd make an omelette if there were some eggs.

d If we didn't have three children, we'd take a year off and travel the world.

e If I were cleverer, I'd be a doctor.

f He'd be a wealthy man if he didn't spend all his money gambling.

g If I had some spare time, I'd learn Russian.

h Jim would have time to spend with his family if he didn't work so hard.

i If I didn't have a headache, I'd be able to go swimming./... I could go ...

j If we had a big house, we'd be able to invite friends to stay./... we could invite ...

6 First or second conditional?

a	rains	won't be able
b	see	will give
c	had	would take up
d	were/was	could
e	don't have	will go
f	were	would go
g	have	will come
h	could	would open
i	is	will you buy
j	had	would soon disappear

7 Correcting mistakes

a I'll make some tea when everyone arrives.

b If I see Peter, I'll tell him to phone you.

c If you aren't careful, you'll lose your money.

d When I go back to my country, I'll write to you.

e If I could travel round the world, I'd go to Hawaii.

f If you came from my country, you would understand what I'm saying.

8 *I'd rather ...*

(Sample answers)

a I'd rather travel by train.

b I'd rather have a winter holiday.

c I'd rather have fizzy mineral water.

d I'd rather watch the football match.

e I'd rather have French fries.

wish and *If only ...*

9 Wishing about the present and past

a You're out of work.

b There's nothing good on TV tonight.

c You like chocolate very much.

d You can't lose weight.

e You didn't win the lottery.

f You left school at sixteen.

g You didn't go to university.

h Your girlfriend didn't ring you last night.

10 A life of regrets

(Sample answers)

a hadn't won

b hadn't given him any money

c could

d would

e hadn't left

f could make some friends

g could go back to my old life

Vocabulary

11 Money

Exercise 1

Nouns
currency   accountant   millionaire
cash dispenser   stockbroker
spending spree   economy   credit card
safe   waste   loan   salary   wages
savings   win   will   bet   coins   cashier

Verbs
squander   waste   earn   loan   invest
win   save   bet

Adjectives
penniless   economical   wealthy
bankrupt   well-off   economic
hard up   safe   broke

Exercise 2

a broke
b safe
c economic
d invested
e coin
f an accountant
g bet
h wasted
i well-off
j salary is
k will

Pronunciation

12 Ways of pronouncing -oo-

/u:/ as in soon = food spoon pool
pools foolishly room bathroom
cool afternoon stool roof

/ʊ/ as in book = good cooks wooden
look football booked took
woollen stood

/ʌ/ as in flood = blood flooded

13 Ways of pronouncing -ou-

Exercise 1

a neighbour
b shoulder
c country
d drought
e cough
f mouse
g doubt
h though

Exercise 2

a thought counts
b enormous mouse
c trouble neighbours
d ought cough
e doubt furious
f Although drought

Multi-word verbs

14 Multi-word verbs with more than one meaning

a work out
b Hang on
c Make up
d going on
e Hang on
f put off our meeting/put our meeting off
g get over
h make it up
i work out
j put me off eating
k get over
l go on

Unit 9

Modal verbs of probability in the present

1 Matching

a They must be tired. They've been travelling all night.
b You can't be hungry after such a huge meal.
c She must be Scottish with a surname like McKenzie.
d He can't be Scottish with a name like Heinrich.
e You must feel very relaxed after your holiday.
g They must know each other well. He's kissed her six times!
h He can't be coming. It's after ten o'clock.
i You must be joking! No one buys two Rolls Royces!
j They can't be getting married! She can't stand him.

2 Why is he late?

Exercise 1

a He must be ill.
b He might be in the coffee bar.
c He could have a dental appointment.
d He may be stuck in a traffic jam.
e His train might be late.
f He must want to miss the test.

Exercise 2 (Sample answers)

a He can't be ill because I spoke to him this morning.
b He can't be in the coffee bar because it's shut.
c He can't have a dental appointment because he had one yesterday.
d He can't be stuck in a traffic jam because he comes by train.
e His train can't be late because it's always on time.
f He can't want to miss the test because he always does so well.

3 Continuous infinitives

a be doing   be having
b be holding   be going
c be sitting
d be using
e be digging   be looking   be looking

Modal verbs of probability in the past

4 must have ..., might have ..., may have ... (Sample answers)

b He must have had an accident.
c He must have got lost.
d She might have been on a long walk. She might have got her feet wet.
e They must have had an argument.
f He might have been to a party.
g They may have won a big prize.
h She must have forgotten her umbrella.

5 Changing sentences

Exercise 1

a You can't have worked hard for your exams.
b They could have gone to Paris.
c I might have left my umbrella on the train.
d He can't have bought another new car.
e She must have been on a diet.
f They could have got married in secret.
g I can't have won the lottery.
h He may have called while we were out.

Exercise 2 (Sample answers)

a ... because you would have done better.
b ... because they said they might be going.
c ... because I definitely had it when I left work.
d ... because he's only just bought one.
e ... because she's certainly lost weight.
f ... because they're both wearing rings!
g ... because I've heard nothing.
h ... because he said he'd call this evening.

6 A poem

Exercise 2

a ☒ He must have left her.
   ☑ She must have left him.

b ❓ They can't have been husband and wife.
   ☑ They definitely lived together.

c ☑ They must have been together for a long time.
   ☒ They can't have been together for a long time.

d ☒ He might be glad she's gone.
   ☑ He must be missing her very much.

e ☑ The house must seem very quiet.
   ❓ He might have pets to keep him company.

f ❓ He must have done something to upset her.
   ☑ She has definitely done something to upset him.

g ☒ He can't be using the bathroom much.
   ☑ He might be trying to avoid using the bathroom.

h ☑ She must have spent a lot of time in the bathroom.
   ☑ The bathroom might have been her favourite room.

i ☑ He might be sleeping downstairs.
   ❓ He can't be sleeping in their old bedroom.

Vocabulary

7 Verbs and nouns that go together

Exercise 1

a plant   f chop
b pick   g crush
c pour   h squeeze
d tear   i twist
e wipe   j rub

Exercise 2

a 3 squeeze   i 1 pouring
b 2 wipe   j 2 rubbing
c 1 tore   k 1 plant
d 2 crushed   l 2 pick
e 3 picked   m 1 crushed
f 1 squeeze   n 3 squeeze
g 3 twist   o 1 tore
h 2 chop

Pronunciation

8 Connected speech

a He can't have arrived early.
b You must have been in Africa.
c They must be coming soon.
d She might have been angry.
e He could have gone abroad.
f She may be arriving this afternoon.
g They can't have been in love.
h They might have eaten it all.

9 Shifting stress

b B Did you say Mr Harper must have left the black suitcase in the taxi?

c B Did you say Mrs Harper must have left the black bag in the taxi?

d B Did you say Mr Harper must have put the black bag in the taxi?

e B Did you say Mr Harper must have left the black bag in the train?

f B Did you say Mr Harper must have left a black bag in the taxi?

g B Did you say Mr Harper might have left the black bag in the taxi?

h B Did you say Mr Harper can't have left the black bag in the taxi?

Prepositions

10 Adjective + preposition

a about   h for   o about
b with   i in   p of
c at   j to   q for
d to   k of   r about
e of   l for   s for
f from   m of   t with
g of   n of

Unit 10

Present Perfect Continuous

1 Present Perfect Simple or Continuous?

Exercise 1

a lost   seen   g never read
b has been eating   h known
c been waiting   i been painting
d crashed   j painted
e have you done   k been having
f been running   l had

Exercise 2

a have been working   haven't finished
b have visited
c has taken   have been looking haven't found
d have been shopping   haven't bought
e have ever read
f have you been doing
   have been working
g has been raining
h have been listening
   haven't understood
i have been reading
j have been trying   have lost
k have been swimming

2 Questions

a How long has he been a singer?
   How many records has he made?

b How long have you been learning (to drive)?
   Have you bought a car yet?

c How long has she been a teacher?
   How many schools has she worked in?

d How long have you been waiting?

e How many people have they invited?
   How long has she known Andrew?

f What have you been doing all this time?
   Where have you been ?

g How many times has Peter been to the States?

h How long have they been going to France for their holidays?

i Where has your mother gone on holiday?

j Has it stopped raining yet ?

Continuous aspect

3 Matching

a 2   g 2   m 1
b 1   h 1   n 2
c 1   i 1   o 2
d 2   j 2   p 1
e 1   k 1
f 2   l 2

4 Simple or Continuous?

a comes
b is coming
c works
d has been working/has worked
e has had
f had
g wants
h is thinking
i think
j to find
k be working
l went
m woke   was raining
n is taking   has
o to go
p be sitting

Time expressions

5 When Sally met Harry

a When was Harry born?
  In 1970.

b How long did he study at
  Loughborough Grammar School?
  Until he was eighteen.

c How long was he at university?
  Three years.

d How long did he go out with Suzie?
  For four years.

e How long did he live in Paris?
  Six months.

f Where did he meet Sally?
  At a party.

g How long has he been working in the
  record shop?
  Since 1994.

h How long has he been manager?
  Since Autumn 1995.

i When did he marry Sally?
  On 23 March 1995.

j How long have they had a house in
  Wimbledon?
  Since 1996.

k How long did Sally live in Canada?
  Until she was fifteen.

l How long has she been interested in
  drama?
  Since she was 11.

m When did she meet Paul?
  While she was working in Poland.

n When did she get married for the first
  time?
  In 1991.

o When was Polly born?
  On 13 May 1992.

p How long was Sally married to Paul?
  For two years.

q How long has she been married to
  Harry?
  Since 1995.

r How long has she been working in
  the school in London?
  Since September 1993.

s When did she meet Harry?
  At Christmas time in 1993.

Vocabulary

6 Suffixes and prefixes

Exercise 1

b thoughtful   thoughtless
c disagree   agreeable   agreement
d careful   careless
e hopeful   hopeless
f unconscious
g inhuman   humanity
h successful
i impolite   politeness
j helpful   helpless
k misunderstand   understandable
l distaste   tasteful   tasteless
m illegal   legality
n illogical   logicality
o distress   stressful
p unpopular   popularity
q misuse   disuse   useful   useless
r unlike   dislike   likeable   likeness

Exercise 2

a hopeless
b unconscious
c Politeness
d inhuman
e disagreement(s)
f unpopular
g misunderstand
h helpful
i likeable   impolite
j illogical
k careful   useless
l distress   thoughtless

Prepositions

7 Prepositions of time

a at   f For
b for   from   to   g Until
c During   at   h in
d in   on   i at
e since   j At

Pronunciation

8 Diphthongs

Exercise 1

a clear   beer
b where   bear
c stay   weigh
d know   phone
e high   shy
f enjoy   noise
g now   aloud
h sure   poor

Exercise 2

a plane   south   Spain
b boy   coat   enjoyed
c known   nearly   five
d wearing   rose   hair
e smoke   pipes   days
f likes   ride   motorbike

Unit 11

Indirect questions

1 Yes/No questions

Exercise 1

a Is   e Has
b Do   f Have
c Did   g Does
d Was   h Did

Exercise 2
(Sample answers)

b I think all birds lay eggs.
c I don't know if dinosaurs laid eggs.
d I don't know if John F. Kennedy was
  the youngest American president.
e I don't think there has ever been a
  female president of the USA.
f I'm not sure if the Olympic Games
  have been held in the same city more
  than once.
g I think Switzerland has a president.
h I'm not sure if William Shakespeare
  lived in London.

Correct answers

a Timbuktu is in Africa.
b All birds lay eggs.
c Dinosaurs did lay eggs.
d John F. Kennedy was not the
  youngest American president.
  Theodore Roosevelt was.
e There has never been a female
  president of the USA.
f The Olympic Games have been held
  in London twice, in 1908 and 1948.
g Yes, Switzerland does have a president.
h Yes, William Shakespeare did once
  live in London.

2 Wh- questions

Exercise 1

a Where   e What
b What   f Who
c Which   g When
d Who   h Which

Exercise 2 (Sample answers)

a I don't know where the word *alphabet* comes from.
b I can't remember what kind of weather the Beaufort Scale measures.
c I'm not sure which countries the Danube flows through.
d I can't remember who the first man in space was./... who was the first man in space.
e I've no idea what NASA stands for.
f I don't know who Adolf Hitler married.
g I've no idea when Margaret Thatcher became Prime Minister.
h I don't know which Latin American country Montezuma II ruled.

Correct answers

a The word *alphabet* comes from Greek.
b The Beaufort Scale measures wind.
c The Danube flows through nine countries: Germany, Austria, Slovakia, Hungary, Croatia, Serbia, Bulgaria, Romania, and Ukraine.
d Yuri Gagarin was the first man in space.
e NASA stands for National Aeronautics and Space Administration.
f Adolf Hitler married Eva Braun.
g Margaret Thatcher became Prime Minister in 1979.
h Montezuma II ruled Mexico in the 16th century.

3 Do you know where ...?

a Could you tell me what time it is?/ ... the time is?
b You're always forgetting where you have put them/your glasses.
c We haven't decided what we are going to give them yet.
d I can't remember whether I posted it/your letter or not.
e I've no idea whose pen it/that is.
f I'm not sure if I'm coming (on the boat trip).
g Do you know who Carol White is?
h I haven't a clue how much he/Jack weighs.

i No idea, but I'd love to know where he gets it all/all his money from.
j Have you any idea how much you spend on clothes?

4 Newspaper headlines

a We don't know exactly how old he is.
b I wonder how he's going to celebrate his birthday.
c Nobody knows how he managed to get out.
d I wonder who helped him to escape.
e I didn't know she'd been married so many times.
f I wonder what went wrong with her last marriage.
g I'd like to know what the score was.
h The headline doesn't say who they were playing against.
i I wonder where he was going to fly to.
j I wonder if he was trying to smuggle drugs.

5 Visiting a town

Exercise 2

a Do you know what the population of Sydney is?
b I've no idea what the name of the harbour is.
c I wonder when Captain Cook sailed to the area.
d I wonder what sort of city Sydney is.
e Do you know when the Harbour Bridge was built?
f Could you tell me where the city centre is?
g I've no idea when the Opera House was opened.
h I haven't a clue who designed it.
i Could you tell me where the best place to go shopping is? /... where is the best place to go shopping?
j Do you know where the Post Office is?
k I wonder what the climate in New South Wales is like.
l Do you happen to know what time tourist offices open?

Exercise 3

1	d	7	j
2	c	8	i
3	h	9	a
4	l	10	e
5	b	11	g
6	k	12	f

Questions with a preposition at the end

6 Who did you speak to?

Exercise 1

a Who are you waiting for?
b Who does he work for?
c What are you thinking about?
d Who did you stay with?
e Who does the pen belong to?
f Who is the letter from?
g What did he die of?
h What are you worried about?
i What are you staring at?
j Who are you writing to?

Exercise 2

a What about?
b Where to?
c What for?
d Who with?
e What about?/What for?
f What about?
g What for?
h Who to?
i What about?
j What with?

Question tags

7 Complete the tag

a do you   f will you
b aren't you   g do we
c didn't we   h aren't I
d isn't it   i have you
e can you   j did they

8 Situations

Exercise 1

a You don't want to go, do you?
b You had too much to drink, didn't you?
c That dress is lovely, isn't it?
d You aren't enjoying this, are you?
e That was superb, wasn't it?

Exercise 2

a Larry, you couldn't lend me five pounds, could you?
b Kate, you don't know where my car keys are, do you?
c Tricia, you haven't got a Russian dictionary, have you?
d Sue, you haven't seen Bill, have you?
e Excuse me, you couldn't change a five-pound note, could you?

Exercise 3

In Exercise 1, the tags go down; in Exercise 2 they go up.

9 Dialogues

a **A** I can't do this exercise. It's very difficult, isn't it?
   B Don't worry. I'm here to help you.
   A I'll be able to do it if I practise, won't I?
   B Of course. It took me ages to learn.

b **A** The Browns have got loads of money, haven't they?
   B I know. They're always going on holiday.
   A I don't know where they get it from.
   B Still, we're happy with what we've got, aren't we?

c **A** You aren't going out dressed like that, are you?
   B Why not? I can wear what I want, can't I?
   A That depends. You're wearing my jacket, aren't you?
   B No, I'm not. I bought this yesterday.

d **A** Dave's new car is great, isn't it?
   B Yes, it's lovely. But he drives much too fast, doesn't he?
   A Yes, it's true.
   B You wouldn't like one like that, would you?
   A Yes, I would. I'd give anything to have a car like that.

Vocabulary

10 Animal idioms

Exercise 1

a to smell a rat
b to set the cat amongst the pigeons
c to behave like a bull in a china shop
d to sort out the sheep from the goats
e to make an ass of yourself
f to talk until the cows come home
g to be as gentle as a lamb
h to be unable to say boo to a goose
i to have a stag party
j to be like water off a duck's back

Exercise 2

a … until the cows came home.
b … the sheep from the goats.
c … stag party.
d … gentle as a lamb.
e … a rat.
f … water off a duck's back.
g … an ass of myself.
h … a bull in a china shop.
i … the cat amongst the pigeons.
j … boo to a goose.

Pronunciation

11 A poem

Exercise 2

a lamb, a goat, a cow
a pig as he went by
a duck, a goose, a hen
a quack, a baa, an oink, a moo

Animal noises
quack: a duck; baa: a sheep; oink: a pig;
moo: a cow

12 Onomatopoeic words

a snores   e banged
b whisper   f smashed
c screamed   g scratched
d groaning   h whistling

Multi-word verbs

13 Common multi-word verbs

Exercise 2

a going on
b set off
c came across
d put up with
e takes up
f Carry on with
g pick you up
h told him off
i let me down
j fallen out
k Come on
l keeps on

Unit 12

Reported statements and questions

1 An argument

Exercise 2

Brian It's your fault that we went to Barbados. It cost a fortune and it was the worst holiday I've ever had.

Thelma There's nothing wrong with Barbados – it's very beautiful. It's the travel firm that's to blame. Their brochure promised all kinds of things about the hotel. And they were all lies. (Crying) You've no right to blame me.

Brian I'm sorry, Thelma. I know it's not really your fault. I'll go to the travel agent first thing in the morning and I'll tell them about everything that went wrong.

Thelma I'll go, too, because I'm going to ask for our money back or another holiday.

2 But you said …

a would fly/would get   d led
b was   e were
c had   f would have

3 Reporting words and thoughts

Exercise 1

a She said she was going to Paris soon.
b I thought the film would be interesting.
c She said she couldn't help me because she had too much to do.
d I was told Ann had bought the tickets.
e She said she thought it was a stupid idea and it wouldn't work.
f The receptionist explained that breakfast was served between 7.00 and 9.00.
g He boasted that he'd been to Oxford University in the 60s.
h She told me she'd never been to America.

Exercise 2

a She asked me if I wanted to go out for a meal.
b They wondered why she was late.
c He asked me if he could use my phone.
d The customs officer asked me where I'd come from.
e She wanted to know how long I was going to be on holiday.
f She asked me when I had to go to work.
g Penny wondered if I'd posted her letter.
h He asked her if she'd be back early.

Exercise 3

a How much do you want?
b And why do you need it?
c What do you do?
d how much do you earn?
e Are you married?
f Have you got any children?
g How long have you lived there?
h When would you like the money?

Exercise 4

a First he asked Mrs Smith how much she wanted.
b Then he wanted to know why she needed it.
c He needed to know what she did.
d She had to tell him how much she earned.
e Then he asked if she was married.
f For some reason, he wanted to know how many children she had.

g He asked her how long she had lived in her flat.

h Finally he wondered when she would like the money.

Reported commands

4 *She advised me to ...*
a She asked Tom to do her a favour.

b The teacher told the class to hand in their essays next week/the following week.

c My wife reminded me to post the letter.

d Rosie invited John to have dinner with them.

e The judge ordered Edward Fox to pay a fine of one hundred pounds.

f Betty persuaded Jane to buy the red dress.

g Gill encouraged Henry to paint professionally.

h She begged me not to tell her father.

i His accountant advised Bill to sell his shares.

ask and *tell*

5 Statements, questions and commands
a She told him to leave her alone.

b He asked her not to go.

c He told Anne he was going to bed.

d Jeremy asked his father how much he earned.

e The teacher told the class to shut up.

f The secretary asked Mr Brown to phone back later.

g The teacher told everyone they had done very well in the test.

h The park keeper told the children not to walk on the grass.

i Sally asked Bill if he was ready to go.

j John told his daughters it was time to get up.

6 Other reporting verbs
a Peter agreed to lend Ann his car.

b Bill admitted that he had stolen the money.

c But Bill denied that he had hit the old lady.

d The professor boasted that he could speak eleven languages perfectly.

e Angela promised to leave work early.

f Henry complained that his soup was cold.

g Jane refused to help me with my homework.

h Kate offered to give Megan a lift to the station.

i Mark suggested that James met him on Thursday, and James agreed.

speak and *talk*

7 A conversation
a talked
b told
c asked
d said/replied
e asked
f explained
g tell
h speak
i replied/said
j tell
k speak
l said
m talk
n said

Vocabulary

8 Birth, death and marriage
Exercise 1
a born
b birthday
c born
d birth
e birth
f birth
g birthday

Exercise 2
a died
b death
c died
d die
e dead die
f dying
g death
h dead
i died dead
j die die dead

Exercise 3
a married   get married
b married
c marry/get married
d been married
e marry
f got married
g got married
h married
i get married

Multi-word verbs

9 Multi-word verbs with two particles
a out of
b down on
c on with
d away from
e down on
f out of
g on with
h up with
i back on
j forward to

Pronunciation

10 Word stress
a funeral
b invite
c invitation
d offer
e argue
f argument
g divorced
h sympathy
i engaged
j godmother
k congratulate
l celebration
m impatient
n confident
o contradict
p forever

11 *had* or *would*?
a She said that she'd seen him. (had)

b She said that she'd see him soon. (would)

c They asked if we'd give them a lift. (would)

d They asked if we'd given her the book. (had)

e He told her he'd loved her a long time. (had)

f He told her he'd love her forever. (would)

g We asked when they'd met each other. (had)

h We asked when they'd meet each other again. (would)

Oxford University Press
Great Clarendon Street, Oxford OX2 6DP

Oxford   New York

Auckland   Bangkok   Buenos Aires   Cape Town
Chennai   Dar es Salaam   Delhi   Hong Kong   Istanbul
Karachi   Kolkata   Kuala Lumpur   Madrid   Melbourne
Mexico City   Mumbai   Nairobi   São Paulo   Shanghai
Taipei   Tokyo   Toronto

OXFORD and OXFORD ENGLISH are trade marks of
Oxford University Press

ISBN 0 19 470225 1   International Edition
ISBN 0 19 436926 9   German Edition

© Oxford University Press 1996

First published 1996
Sixteenth impression 2003
German Edition first published 1999
Fourth impression 2003

Printed in Spain by Mateu Cromo, S.A. Pinto (Madrid)

**The authors and publisher are grateful for permission
to reproduce the following copyright material.**

p 56 'The house is not the same since you left' by
  Henry Normal, reprinted by permission of Bloodaxe
  Books Ltd from *Nude Modelling for the Afterlife*
  (Bloodaxe Books, 1993)

Illustrations by:

Julie Anderson pp 6, 17, 25, 29, 44, 75
Nicki Elson pp 11, 18, 51, 73
Rosamund Fowler pp 9, 26, 30, 32, 33, 48, 56, 57, 78
Clive Goodyer pp 34, 40
Madeleine Hardie pp 8, 9, 52, 61
Ian Kellas pp 5, 14, 27, 38, 53, 58
Christine Pilsworth pp 31, 36, 62, 77
Philip Reeve pp 13, 19, 32, 50, 54, 55, 69
Harry Venning pp 25, 64, 71

**The Publishers would like to thank the following for
their kind permission to reproduce photographs and
other copyright material:**

The Bridgeman Art Library pp 42 (Giraudon –
  Van Gogh), 43 (Tate Gallery – *A Bigger Splash*
  [1967] © David Hockney 1967)
Mary Evans Picture Library pp 42 (*Jane Austen*), 65
The Image Bank pp 24 (M Melford – *gardener*, E Sulle –
  teenager, R Lockyer – *businesswoman*), 37 (G Rossi –
  Masai), 42 (*pop star*), 74 (P F Runyon)
Moderna Museet, Stockholm p 46 (*museum*)
Network p 45 (M Goldwater)
Popperfoto p 21 (*Amy Johnson*)
Range Picture Library pp 20 (Bettmann/UPI),
  21 (Bettmann/UPI – *Blondin*), 42 (Bettmann/UPI –
  Marilyn Monroe)
Redferns p 42 (M Prior – *Bob Marley*)
The Still Moving Picture Company p 46 (*Loch Ness*)
Tony Stone Images pp 37 (R Lynn – *elephant*),
  42 (C Slattery – *writer*, J Dare – *actress*), 54 (P Correz),
  63 (K Fisher – *woman*, D Bosler – *man*),
  68 (E Collacott)

Design by: Holdsworth Associates, Isle of Wight